Careers Unleashed

Unlock your potential for extraordinary career success

ASAD HUSAIN

Re^think

First published in Great Britain in 2023
by Rethink Press (www.rethinkpress.com)

© Copyright Asad Husain

All rights reserved. No part of this publication may be reproduced, stored in or introduced into a retrieval system, or transmitted, in any form, or by any means (electronic, mechanical, photocopying, recording or otherwise) without the prior written permission of the publisher.

The right of Asad Husain to be identified as the author of this work has been asserted by him in accordance with the Copyright, Designs and Patents Act 1988.

This book is sold subject to the condition that it shall not, by way of trade or otherwise, be lent, resold, hired out, or otherwise circulated without the publisher's prior consent in any form of binding or cover other than that in which it is published and without a similar condition including this condition being imposed on the subsequent purchaser.

Cover images © Shutterstock | Elena LAtkun and Natali Snailcat, and Freepik | callmetak

Author photographs © Monika S Jakubowska

With immense love and gratitude, I dedicate this book to my mother (Shireen Husain) and my father (Arif Husain), without whom I would not be who I am and where I am.

To Amber, my wife, whose love, support and partnership has meant everything in this journey of mine.

To my two sons, Arsalan and Amaan, life means so much more with them in it.

To my siblings, Yasmin, Atif, Amir, and Shazia, for always being there for me.

To all my leaders, peers, subordinates, coaches, coachees and colleagues all over the world, for enriching my career journey.

Contents

Introduction	**1**
My career journey	4
Exceptional careers are not built on chance	5
The roadmap to career success	6
1 Relevance	**9**
Relevance, the essence of extraordinary careers	9
The changing career landscape	11
Summary	27
2 Knowing Yourself	**29**
Know yourself	30
The power within: Unraveling your career story	33

Career compass: Finding your 'true north' in direction and drive	36
Inner kaleidoscope: Discovering the multifaceted aspects of yourself in career exploration	41
Core compass: Discovering your guiding values	44
Summary	50

3 Strategies To Bulletproof Your Career — **53**

Futureproof your career: Embrace lifelong learning for lasting relevance	54
Career by design: Proactively craft your path to success	58
Follow your 'north star': Let your aspiration guide your career journey	61
Multiply your opportunities: Harness the networking advantage for career growth	63
Summary	67

4 Mindset For Career Success — **69**

The four critical mindset types	71
Summary	86

5 Career-Building And Navigation Power Skills — **87**

Why do you need power skills?	88
Mastering the skill of creating impact	93

Stacking meaningful experiences	96
Performance leverage advantage	97
Reskilling and upskilling for career relevancy	99
Connecting today with your future by taking action	101
Summary	102

6 Your Career Development Plan — **103**

Career aspiration	107
Long- and short-term goals	110
Strengths and areas of improvement (2:1 ratio)	111
Action steps	116
Summary	117

7 Important Career Conversations — **119**

The four types of career conversations	120
Summary	132

Conclusion — **135**

The Author — **139**

Introduction

If you are reading this, chances are you are stuck at average, yet you aspire to an outstanding career.

You wake up each morning wanting extraordinary success and fulfillment and are looking for the key to unlock and achieve your full career potential.

You are hungry to deliver value and make an impact. You want to thrive in your career consistently.

You see some people achieve remarkable career success and fulfillment, you see them thriving and you wonder how they got there and what you need to do to get there too.

If you are looking to create an exceptional career that brings you both success and fulfillment, whether you are just starting out in your career, mid-career, in the middle of a career transition, or looking to take your career to the next level, this book is for you.

My name is Asad Husain and I am incredibly passionate about unleashing your full potential if you are motivated and hungry to make a difference in the world through your career.

I have had the privilege of working with all kinds of professionals in blue chip companies like Exxon, the Gillette Company, Proctor & Gamble, Dun & Bradstreet, Del Monte, C&S Wholesale Grocers, and smaller companies and startups, over a thirty-one-year career, spanning various industries and numerous geographies across the globe. I have had the honor to lead the HR function in four different organizations.

This has enabled me to observe firsthand numerous professionals, managers, leaders and executives build impressive careers while experiencing tremendous change and transformations in their organizations and their industry. And unfortunately, for every person I observed build a fantastic career, I have seen many more feel unsuccessful and unfulfilled in their careers.

My work in Human Resources meant that I was responsible for leading and working with talent management systems and processes in organizations. The intent was to continuously raise the capability

INTRODUCTION

of the organization and the individuals to deliver the business strategy and objectives while engaging and motivating the workforce. This entailed identifying high-potential individuals, helping to decide who gets promoted, coming up with the best development path for individuals, and conducting hundreds of career discussions. This gave me an in-depth view of what works and what does not in the talent space.

My own career started as an HR trainee in Karachi, Pakistan and by all measures, I have had an exceptional career. My career journey enabled me to understand what it takes to succeed and reach the pinnacle of one's profession. In my last job, I was the Chief Human Resources Officer of a $26bn company with 17,000 employees in New Hampshire. In fact, for a year-and-a half, I was also the Chief Human Resources of a second company in Andover, Massachusetts, a startup, splitting time between the two organizations. During my career, I benefited from excellent advice, coaching, and mentorship and learned a great deal from the many mistakes I made. I also learned to develop the courage it takes to push myself out of my comfort zone to grow. My diversified career experience and success gives me a unique understanding of what it takes to be successful.

Throughout my career I strived to make my subordinates successful in their careers. I am proud to report that, thus far, sixteen former subordinates have become Heads of Human Resources of their organizations.

In my last job, we wanted greater career ownership by employees. I designed a four-hour training program based on my career learnings. We received fantastic feedback. Over the next two years, we had almost 550 employees participate in this workshop. This further honed my approach toward helping others succeed in their careers.

My career journey

Around this same time, I began searching for more fulfillment in my career. I had achieved my short- and long-term career goals, which included financial freedom. I was creating significant impact in the two companies as the Head of HR and my family was in a good place. What should my calling be now? I was highly grateful for my career, but I was questioning, 'Why me?' One moment I was a young man starting my career in Pakistan, and now, here I was, successful at a global level.

I did some deep reflection. And it finally hit me. The purpose of my career journey was to prepare me to use my knowledge, skills and experience to help others who also have the hunger and desire to achieve something meaningful. To give them a clear roadmap for their career. I decided to quit my biggest and highest-paying job with the aim to help and inspire others to success and fulfillment and focus on other areas of my life. A month after I left my job, Covid-19

INTRODUCTION

hit the world. I started to receive calls from people regarding their jobs, career options and decisions. Two years later, I decided to write this book.

We live in a world where the future of careers is uncertain, the traditional path to success is dead and fulfillment has become increasingly important. With the world of work changing rapidly, you must take control of your career and create an approach uniquely your own and in sync with your whole self. I have written this book to help you navigate the challenges of the modern workplace and to provide you with the tools and strategies necessary to create an extraordinary career.

Exceptional careers are not built on chance

The belief that it takes luck to have a great career is invalid. Exceptional careers are rarely built on chance and being in the right place at the right time, particularly in a world of work that keeps changing and evolving. It takes a potent and evolving combination of mindset, skills and strategies to construct an exceptional career. Most people worldwide are unhappy with their careers and want to make a change. In its 'State of the Global Workplace Report 2022',[1] Gallup

---

[1] CCA, 'State of the Global Workplace: 2022 Report', (Gallup, 2 May 2023), www.cca-global.com/content/latest/article/2023/05/state-of-the-global-workplace-2022-report-346, accessed 19 June 2023

found that, along with dissatisfaction, workers are experiencing staggering rates of both disengagement and unhappiness:

- 60% reported being emotionally detached at work.
- 19% reported being miserable.
- Only 33% reported feeling engaged.
- In the US, 50% of workers reported feeling stressed at their jobs daily, 41% worried, 22% sad and 18% angry.

This dissatisfaction has been the case for quite a few years. So why are people not doing something about their unhappiness and disengagement at work?

There are two reasons for this. First, they are waiting for something or someone to do something for them to have happiness and success, for the right opportunity to fall in their lap, and for their luck to change. Second, even if they want to act and take ownership of their career success, they do not have the required mindset, strategies and skills.

The roadmap to career success

When you finish reading this book, you will have an authentic roadmap to create an extraordinary career: one that is unique to you. If you follow the steps outlined in each chapter, I guarantee that not only will you achieve your career goals, but you thrive while doing so. Through the compelling stories and vivid examples I share, you will also grasp the concepts of career ownership and manifestation and find inspiration and motivation to shape your career trajectory actively.

You will learn to break free from the sleepwalking mentality that keeps many stuck in unfulfilling careers. This book will give you the tools and knowledge to break free from career monotony and status quo and carve a path toward a fulfilling professional life. You will learn how to overcome the fear of failure, challenge the boundaries of your comfort zone and take the necessary risks toward realizing your true professional potential.

When times are turbulent, like the present, most people hunker down and seek the safety of what they are accustomed to. This presents an excellent opportunity to be different and disruptive and go for what you want in your career. This book shows you how to go about it, not in a reckless manner, but in a profoundly thoughtful, reflective and planned way.

In the chapters that follow, you will discover and understand:

- The essence of continued career success in a rapidly changing world of work is being relevant.

- How knowing yourself leads to inner alignment, which leads to optimum career decision-making.
- Which critical career strategies will bulletproof success for you.
- The mindset you need to succeed.
- The power skills needed to be competent in building successful careers.
- How to put together your career development plan for success.

Careers Unleashed will help you to identify what measure of extraordinary success and fulfillment you want from your career, and how to act to achieve it. It starts with the premise that you want this, but as the adage says, 'You can take a horse to the water, but you can't make it drink.' Each chapter will require you to do some deep, reflective thinking. Please journal your thoughts and answers along the way. I guarantee that this will lead you to an authentic and exciting path for you to follow in pursuance of career success and fulfillment.

Careers Unleashed gives you a comprehensive approach: read it, do the work required and position yourself to make the best possible career decisions. Let's go!

ONE
Relevance

Relevance, the essence of extraordinary careers

It was 9.30am on a cold and crisp morning in St Petersburg, Russia. I was three weeks into my new role as HR Director, Former Soviet Union (fifteen countries) for the Gillette Company. I had moved to Russia from Boston, the world headquarters of the company. I was in the conference room about to begin my presentation on my HR findings thus far. The audience was my CEO and the other members of the leadership team – all expatriates from France, Turkey, Germany and the UK and one of them from Russia. I was very confident. I had done an in-depth analysis of the HR function and started my presentation. There were a few questions and comments by the end, and I was unsure how to interpret that. As we headed for a short break, one of the leaders walking past me said, 'So you came all the way from Boston to tell us all the things we are doing wrong?' I was taken aback by his comments, and it took me the rest of the day to understand an important lesson in my career: *I was right, but I was not relevant.*

As a young, hotshot HR leader from the world headquarters of the Gillette Company, I prepared a presentation on what we needed to fix in HR. The compensation strategy required correction. Training & Development missed the mark. Recruitment needed to do better. All of this was accurate, but my findings seemed irrelevant to the critical problems the leaders were trying to solve. The business required expansion into nearly fifty new cities across fifteen countries. It needed a new manufacturing and warehousing facility, and the consolidation of five Gillette businesses under one structure. My presentation should have mentioned how HR would support and impact these challenges. To be successful in that important position, I needed to have an impact on the business. To have an impact, I needed to be relevant to the business' biggest problems.

If you desire any degree of success in your career, you must demonstrate your relevance to the most significant business problems of today and tomorrow. Your education, knowledge, skills, mindset and experience must help you solve problems that businesses have today and tomorrow. No matter what path you choose for your career, if you are not relevant to the world of work today and where it will head, you will not thrive, or even survive, in your career.

What causes career irrelevance? The most significant cause is when the speed of change around you at work or in your profession is faster than the speed of change within yourself. We are experiencing a world of work where change is continuous, and the pace of change is faster than ever before, moving us faster towards irrelevance.

To counter this, you need to continuously unlearn and relearn by taking multiple dips into acquiring new education, knowledge, skills and experiences to tackle the business problems of today and tomorrow. The more pertinent these are, the higher the probability that you will significantly impact the business. The more significant your impact, the higher your chances of having an extraordinary career.

Does this resonate with you?

The changing career landscape

Let's look deeper at what has changed in the career landscape before determining what needs to change within you.

Over the last three years, almost everything we know about careers changed as we saw significant global disruptions at work, bringing the future forward at an accelerated pace. What we thought would require years to implement and was cost-prohibitive started happening almost overnight. The nature of the Covid-19 pandemic did not cause these accelerated global shifts. These trends existed before 2020, but the pandemic escalated and magnified them. Governments and organizations underwent significant forced and rapid unlearning and relearning and had to take unprecedented steps to survive.

Similarly, almost everything we know about careers has changed during this time, but the trends were also there before. The pandemic intensified them, and the unimaginable and tragic loss of lives across the globe made us pause and reset what is important to us in life and where we are spending our time.

The result is that how we got to where we are in our careers, whether by design, accident or happenstance, will not help us much in getting where we want to go, or maybe even survive, any longer. The playing field and the rules have changed massively. The rethink and reset resulting from the shock and tragedy have caused a regeneration process that will not allow us to return to the way it was. Mandates from the likes of Elon Musk and other CEOs to return to work cannot undo the new relationships and connections we have formed with life, work and what is important to us. New wirings are now in place. Regeneration has taken place.

There are six key career trends that need to be understood before we put together our career game plan.

In this chapter, we will discuss these trends in detail, as without understanding these, you will find it challenging to remain relevant and struggle to take charge of your career.

Career Trend #1: Embracing longer careers

A career is the sum of the time you will spend in all the jobs you will have to earn a living, regardless of your profession, occupation or trade. According to data from Our World in Data, the average number of hours worked per year by full-time workers in the United States in 2017 was approximately 1,757 hours.[2] Assuming you start working at the age of twenty-two and retire at sixty-five, a typical career span would result in you working a total of approximately 75,551 hours over the course of your career. This already seems like a long time.

Now consider two other factors. First, the average life expectancy has been increasing globally over the past few decades, partly due to advances in medical care, improvements in public health infrastructure and decreasing rates of infectious diseases. Although life expectancy numbers in the US fell over the past two years, mainly due to the impact of the pandemic, according to the World Health Organization (WHO),

---

2   C Giattino, E Ortiz-Ospina and M Roser, 'Working Hours', (Our World in Data, first published in 2013, most recent substantial revision December 2020), https://ourworldindata.org/working-hours, accessed 13 July 2023

global life expectancy at birth increased from 67 years in 2000 to 73 years in 2019.[3] Each generation now expects to live longer than their parents. A 2019 report by the United Nations suggests that children born in this century should expect to live to 100 and that the number of people aged 80 years or older is expected to triple by 2050.[4]

Second, people are generally not saving more to account for a possible longer retirement. In the US, people are saving less than they should be for retirement. A 2021 report from the National Institute on Retirement Security stated that experts predict that the economic fallout from the pandemic may create substantial uncertainty about financing retirement, causing Americans to work longer or rethink retirement altogether.[5] If both these trends continue, it will mean that we will have to work more years in our lives. Lynda Gratton, a professor of management practice at the London Business School, has written extensively on the topic of longer careers. In her book, *The 100-Year Life: Living and Working in an Age*

---

3 World Health Organization (WHO), 'World Health Statistics 2023: Monitoring health for the SDGs, sustainable development goals', (WHO, 19 May 2023), www.who.int/publications/i/item/9789240074323, accessed 13 July 2023
4 Department of Economic and Social Affairs, 'World Population Prospects 2019', (United Nations, 2019), https://population.un.org/wpp/publications/files/wpp2019_highlights.pdf, accessed 13 July 2023
5 T Bond, D Doonan and K Kenneally, 'Retirement Insecurity 2021: Americans' views of retirement, (National Institute on Retirement Security, February 2021), www.nirsonline.org/wp-content/uploads/2021/02/FINAL-Retirement-Insecurity-2021-.pdf, accessed 13 July 2023

of Longevity, she argues that people will need to work longer to support longer lifespans, and that sixty-year careers could become the norm.[6]

If careers are going to be up to sixty years, the questions that come up are:

- How many organizations, on average, will people work for during their careers? When my father started work in the early 1960s, he joined a well-established multinational company as a management trainee, expecting to grow within and retire from the same company. He ended up working for three companies in total. I have worked for seven companies in my thirty-one years. My son, who is twenty-six, has already worked for two companies in almost four years.

- How many jobs, on average, will people have in their careers? According to the Bureau of Labor Statistics' September 2022 report on employee tenure, the median job tenure for people in the US aged twenty-five to thirty-four (this includes Millennials) is 2.8 years.[7]

- Will people still want to work the same number of hours on average (75,551) but spread them

---

[6] L Gratton, *The 100-Year Life: Living and Working in an Age of Longevity* (Bloomsbury Publishing, 2 June 2016)

[7] U.S. Bureau of Labor Statistics, 'Economic News Release: Employee Tenure', (US Census Bureau and the BLS, 22 September 2022), www.bls.gov/news.release/tenure.t01.htm, accessed 13 July 2023

over sixty years instead of forty-three years? Maybe work four days a week instead of five?

- Will the college degrees that young adults earn by twenty-two be enough to sustain a possible sixty-year career?

How long will your career be, and how will you stay relevant in a continuously changing world?

Career Trend #2: Mastering strategic choices for happiness at work

Gallup's 'State of the Global Workplace 2022' report on worldwide engagement states that only 21% of employees are engaged. More worrisome is that 19% are, in fact, unhappy.[8] So, 79% of the workforce is either disengaged or unhappy at work. Wow!

There is much to be said about the culture and leadership in organizations contributing to this disengagement and unhappiness, but a significant portion of the disengagement is career related.

My own experience suggests the same. Over my thirty-plus-year career in Human Resources, I have worked with thousands of people across the globe and found most of them unhappy with their careers.

---

8   CCA, 'State of the Global Workplace: 2022 Report', (Gallup, 2 May 2023), www.cca-global.com/content/latest/article/2023/05/state-of-the-global-workplace-2022-report-346, accessed 19 June 2023

They feel stuck, not valued, not recognized, passed over for promotions, have no prospects for growth and need help knowing where to go or what to do. When I have tried to unravel their unhappiness, among other things, career decisions, or lack of, are a significant part of it. This raises the questions:

- Are we making good career decisions that lead to greater engagement and happiness?
- As the numbers suggest, on average, we will work for twelve companies or more and change jobs every three years. Do we have the capability to make good career decisions?

You must make strategic and thoughtful career decisions to avoid long periods of disengagement and unhappiness, not meeting your career expectations and possibly adversely impacting your health, well-being and relationships.

Career Trend #3: Aligning work values for success and fulfillment

Work values are priorities, beliefs, ethics and morals that drive our motivation and behavior at work. For example, a work value may be, 'I am motivated by undertaking new challenges in my job,' or, 'My company inspires me by being environmentally responsible.'

For the first time in history, there are five generations in the workforce. Each generation is defined by different worldviews, communication styles and motivations. An infographic by Purdue Global lists these attributes as motivators to the five generations:

- Traditionalists (1925–1945): Respect, recognition, providing long-term value to the company.
- Baby Boomers (1946–1964): Company loyalty, teamwork, duty.
- Generation X (1965–1980): Diversity, work-life balance, their personal-professional interests rather than the company's interests.
- Millennials or Generation Y (1981–2000): Responsibility, the quality of their manager, unique work experiences.
- Generation Z or Zoomers (2001): Diversity, personalization, individuality, creativity.[9]

Organizations have long grappled with creating a culture and work environment that responds satisfactorily to the generations' varying expectations, but a fundamental shift in the balance of power occurred after the pandemic. Whereas previously, the employer decided where, when and how work would happen (hence defining the work values of

---

9 Purdue Global, 'Generational Differences in the Workplace [Infographic]', (no date), www.purdueglobal.edu/education-partnerships/generational-workforce-differences-infographic, accessed 19 July 2023

their organization), now the balance of power has tilted in favor of the employee. Covid-19 has made us rethink and reset what is important to us in life and how work fits into our lives.

Work-life balance is not enough anymore. The question is much broader now, as employees are also looking for flexibility regarding where and when to work. The pandemic blew away the myths that remote work is not possible at a large scale, will take a long time to implement, and will not be productive. Unlike pre-Covid, a broader section of the workforce now wants this flexibility. Employees also expect some level of control when it comes to flexibility. As they determine their priorities in life, this may differ for different employees. CEOs might require all their employees to return to work, and employees must then decide if they want to work at that organization. Flexibility will tilt the balance for the best in the war for talent.

Additionally, due to this 'rethink and reset', their work no longer determines the identity of a large part of the workforce. Work is a part of their life, but does not equal it. Their title, profession or compensation does not determine their identity. They want to carve out an identity that defines who they are in life. For the employee, understanding one's career aspirations and the work values accompanying it is critical to enable a better and happier life.

Do you have your work values figured out?

Career Trend #4: Navigating the 'jungle gym' of careers

Planning a career has always been important, but never more than now, and preparing for it in today's new world of work requires new thinking. In designing a successful and fulfilling career, we can no longer consider following the traditional linear career path or ladder.

The traditional career ladder, where you earn a degree, join an organization in an entry-level position, and then move up the ladder in predefined steps (jobs), does not work in today's turbulent and exciting workplace. These linear career paths came about because employees needed assistance in navigating increasingly complex organizations, and these prescriptive paths identified steps and the destination for them, often leading to a C-suite or a CEO position. This approach worked when organizations and jobs were relatively stable and there were few new career options, but now the landscape has changed significantly.

In pursuing efficiency and effectiveness, organizations have flattened organizational structures and have eliminated several positions that were once a prescribed 'next step' in the traditional career ladder. The experience and skills gap between a boss and subordinate in most organizations is now much more significant due to the missing rungs in the ladder. A Financial Planning Analyst may report to the company's Chief Financial Officer in a flattened structure, but it is hard to imagine the analyst going directly from her analyst position to the CFO position. She would need additional jobs to enhance her knowledge, skills and experience.

Organizations are also more fluid and dynamic now. New revenue growth avenues, mergers and acquisitions often require new skills and experiences, which leads to a broader set of experiences and skills needed to progress. Artificial Intelligence (AI) is already unpacking tremendous changes in how organizations structure jobs and how work gets done. The movement necessary for career progression in these organizations is more than upwards. It could be sideways or even downwards.

From an employee's perspective, how they view their career has changed and the rigidity of the traditional career ladder no longer works. People are continually moving, changing jobs every three years on average, and working for twelve-plus companies in their careers. Additionally, the Covid-19 'rethink and reset' has led to:

- Many people pivoting to something completely different and new in their careers, but something they enjoy doing.
- Others having side hustles while working day jobs, adventuring into the creator economy.

- More than ever, people are looking for meaning and purpose at work, and their destination may not be the senior leadership position in a company. They define the peak of their career differently. According to the Ivanti Survey (2021), 63% of respondents in the US and 66% in the UK would choose the ability to work from anywhere over getting a promotion.[10]

Given the above dynamics of the turbulent workplace and how employees see their careers, if the linear ladder is outdated, how should you think about career progression?

In her book *Lean In: Women, Work, and the Will to Lead*, Sheryl Sandberg, chief operating officer of Facebook, encourages women to pursue their career goals by embracing a non-linear path and taking risks. She describes career paths today as a 'jungle gym': you swing from one bar to another sideways, upwards and downwards. There is no prescribed path; you have the freedom to put together moves that make sense to you and have fun while doing it.[11] You need a broader set of experiences to understand how various parts of the organization connect to be more impactful versus a linear path. You need multiple perspectives to enhance your ability to navigate and collaborate to get things done.

---

10   Ivanti, 'Everywhere Workplace Survey Results', (Ivanti, May 2021), www.ivanti.com/company/everywhere-workplace-survey-results, accessed 13 July 2023
11   S Sandberg, *Lean In: Women, Work, and the Will to Lead* (WH Allen, 12 March 2013)

As you live longer, stay healthier for longer and possibly have a longer career, it's unlikely you will follow the current life stages of learning up to the age of twenty-one or twenty-two, working until sixty-five and then retiring for twenty years. You may follow a different path: learn, work, learn, work, sabbatical, work and retire, or some permutation of this. With career progression no longer linear and careers potentially lasting up to sixty years, the importance of exploration and self-discovery becomes even more critical.

In the career jungle gym, multiple paths and opportunities will be available throughout your career, allowing you to explore different roles, industries and interests. You will need to discover what you want, seek out new experiences, experiment with different paths and make informed choices about your career trajectory.

You will need to be more adept at navigating changes in the job market, technological advancements and evolving industry trends. By taking the time to discover what you want, you can intentionally acquire skills that will serve you well in multiple contexts, enhancing your long-term career prospects.

Swinging from one opportunity to another in the career jungle gym will require learning from each experience, reassessing progression and being open to new possibilities. It also means that career exploration and self-discovery will need to be a continuous process.

Career Trend #5: The expanding career horizon

Another significant trend impacting the world of work and careers is the number and diversity of career options available.

From an organizational perspective, the speed of this continuous change requires rapid capability building. Organizations do not have time to build most of the capability by grooming and developing talent. Talent competition and employee retention make this task even harder. These challenges have forced organizations to fill their talent needs with a much more expansive approach. They are building workforce plans with different 'Human Resources' categories and expanding their talent pool for their needs. The illustration below lists some of these types of resources.

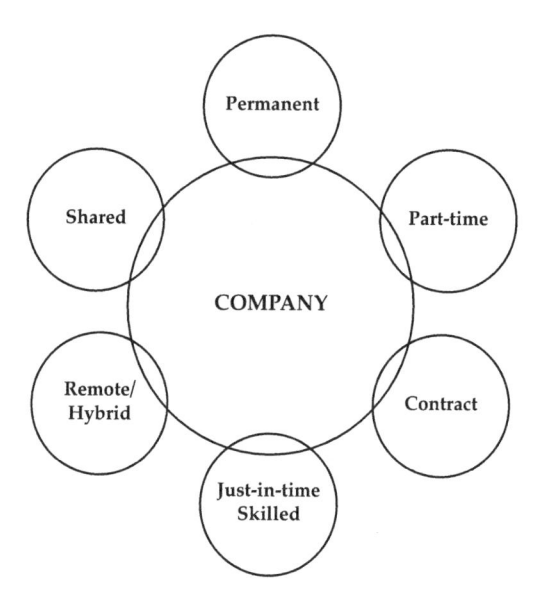

- Permanent
- Part-time
- Contract
- Just-in-time Skilled
- Remote/Hybrid
- Shared

COMPANY

From an employee perspective, this opens up more options. They can opt for a different category of employment that suits them at various points in their careers.

With organizations laying off employees in more challenging times, many people are protecting themselves by offering their skills to several companies rather than working for just one organization at a time. Instead of protecting their job against layoffs, they are building career employability – a win-win for both the organization and the employee. For example, I know of a doctor in the Michigan area in the US being shared among several hospitals across different states. The doctor is happy because this provides additional exposure and learning. The hospitals are delighted because, instead of battling limited talent pools for expensive talent, they have access to the best talent at a reasonable cost. A shared resource with a shared cost, it's a win-win for the hospitals and the doctor.

The above options are about how people want to show up for work at different career stages. Add to this mix the changes that automation, digitization and AI bring to the world of work and the career landscape.

You must reimagine all your career options and be ready to reinvent yourself to pursue some of them. I encourage you to open your mind to having a career in multiple disciplines, functions, and capacities (for example, employee, owner, creator, advisor), interjected with several stints in learning.

Career Trend #6: Skills as the currency of success

The world of work has changed and continues to do so at warp speed. Early in the pandemic, it was mostly about business continuity and survival, but now organizations are focused on thriving in this ever-changing environment.

Whereas jobs used to be central to organizational design, the focus is now on upskilling and reskilling the workforce. To succeed, organizations are becoming much more fluid and adapting with speed to a continually changing landscape.

The 'Future of Jobs Report' in 2020 by the World Economic Forum states that the accelerated automation and the economic uncertainty due to the pandemic will result in a shift in the division of labor between humans and machines which will lead to 85 million jobs being displaced and 97 million new jobs being created by the year 2025.[12] As jobs disappear and new jobs appear, organizations and people need to respond through reskilling and upskilling. Organizations that do not do this will not survive, and people who do not unlearn and relearn in terms of skills will become redundant. Skills are the new currency at work.

---

12 World Economic Forum, 'The Future of Jobs Report 2020', (World Economic Forum, October 2020), www3.weforum.org/docs/WEF_Future_of_Jobs_2020.pdf, accessed 13 July 2023

The implication for careers is that you will need to grow, evolve and reinvent yourself continuously in terms of skills. The shelf life of most skills is decreasing quickly. These are the questions you should consider:

- Do you have a lifelong learning mindset?
- Are you open to acquiring new skills and updating existing ones to remain competitive?
- Do you have the ability to learn and apply new skills quickly?
- Are you diversifying your skillset?
- Which transferable skills can help you stay relevant?

Summary

In this chapter, I have highlighted six key career trends, but what does all of this mean to you in creating your future career path?

- There is very little predictability to career paths today.
- Work is no longer just work; it has a lot more meaning and purpose attached to it for all of us.
- You must make a mental shift towards a continuous reinvention of yourself to remain relevant and, therefore, employable.

- With so many options, choices and continuous change, you must own your career. Take charge of it regarding what you want, and how to get it.

- Being in charge of your career means you are proactive, aware of trends, and adapt as you go along. Sleepwalking for long periods in jobs is not going to be possible.

- Your success in your career will equal your personal development and growth.

- Having clarity on how to construct a career that leads you to success and fulfillment is critical.

- You need to elevate your career strategy and plan for this new landscape.

I pointed out that you become irrelevant when the change outside is faster than the change within you. In this chapter, we have covered what is changing on the outside by describing the most important trends in the workplace and their impact on careers. I suggest taking time to reflect on these two questions. Taking the time to journal them will be most effective:

- Have the circumstances, events and overall change over the last three years impacted how you think about your career? How?

- Has what has been important to you in your career changed during the last three years? Why?

The next chapter is all about looking within you.

TWO
Knowing Yourself

In Chapter 1, we understood that the essence of career success is being relevant to the business problems of today and tomorrow. The external world around you is changing. This chapter deals with inner discovery and alignment so that you understand what you need to keep, change, renew and acquire within yourself, to remain relevant and achieve career success and fulfillment. We will focus on four elements of knowing and understanding yourself better:

1. The power within: Unraveling your career story

2. Career compass: Finding your 'true north' in direction and drive

3. Inner kaleidoscope: Discovering the multifaceted aspects of yourself in career exploration
4. Core compass: Discovering your guiding values

To begin any journey, you must know where you are starting your journey from. If I tell you that you need to go to Boston, the first thing you need to know is where you are right now. Are you in New York, Warsaw, Tokyo or Toronto? That will help you determine how you will get to Boston, ie, take a plane, bus, train, car or just walk. When it comes to careers, we frequently identify where we want to get to, often in the distant future, without truly understanding where we are starting our journey from.

Know yourself

The first step in your career planning journey is knowing yourself in detail. You need to start with this step to recognize, appreciate and leverage the choices and opportunities that come your way. If you do not start with this, you put yourself at a significant disadvantage. As Dumbledore wisely tells Harry in JK Rowling's book *Harry Potter and the Chamber of Secrets*, 'It is our choices, Harry, that show what we truly are, far more than our abilities.'[13] Knowing yourself is the foundation of being able to make good

---

13 JK Rowling, *Harry Potter and the Chamber of Secrets* (Scholastic Press, 1999); Chapter 18 – Dobby's Reward

choices in your career. When constructing extraordinary careers, you need both capability building and decision-making, but where most people falter is the decision-making part.

Let me share a good example. A few years back, I was having a development discussion with a high-potential leader. He was very ambitious about his career progression and mentioned that he wanted to be in a CEO position by a certain age. He had ruffled a few feathers in the leadership group by saying that he would have to make it happen elsewhere if it did not happen in the company he worked for. As he and I sat down to talk, my opening question was, 'Why the CEO position?' What would the CEO position give him? Power? Money? Influence? Status? I could see he was a little surprised by that question. He had not given it much thought; whatever he said to me was just his immediate response. He told me that having the CEO position would give him 'power, money and influence', and he wanted all that. My follow-up question was, 'What if the company gave you the money, power and influence, but not the CEO title? Would that be OK with you?' I saw him shift in his seat again, indicating he was unsure how to answer my question.

He had clearly identified a narrow career goal for himself, a title, but had yet to fully reflect much on why that title, and why by a certain age. He was stating his career choices without much deep self-reflection. He had the potential to be a future CEO, but did not know *why* he wanted that position. As a result, he was unclear on what roles or achievements would help him to get there. All he knew was that he needed bigger roles and some time. During our subsequent discussions, I helped him understand that without deep self-reflection, he had identified a narrow career goal, attached an arbitrary timeline to that career goal, and was perhaps closing many doors on himself. There was no guarantee that, even if he acquired the CEO title at this company (or any other company), it would give him the money, power or influence that he sought.

With so much change in the world of work, you need to regularly self-reflect on what you want from your career, and why. If you do not do that, you will not be able to leverage the evolving career options and enjoy a successful and fulfilling career. I have observed many professionals across the globe stumble and take missteps in their careers because they have yet to truly understand what is important to them at various stages of their careers. They assign a shallow, artificial, or kind of 'what's expected of me', narrow career goal for themselves and make career decisions based on that. They often get stuck, disillusioned and disappointed in their careers. They wonder why all the opportunities go to others and explain it away by saying to themselves that they are not lucky.

Have you thoroughly reflected on what you want from your career, and why?

The power within: Unraveling your career story

This is the first element of getting to know yourself that I use when working with my clients. What is your career story? When professionals come to me for career coaching, I ask them to tell me their career stories thus far in their own words. I ask them to be brief and only to let me know what got them to this point in their careers and how they see where their career stands at that moment. What I am looking out for is how they tell their story. What do they emphasize, and what do they leave out of their career story? Later, I ask them to write it down, limiting it to around 200 words. By writing it down, my clients and I can assess the story better. They get the opportunity to see their thoughts, beliefs and feelings before them versus these just rolling around in their heads, causing confusion.

The stories we tell ourselves internally become our reality because we keep repeating them to ourselves, believe them, and tend to operate within them. These stories heavily influence what we think we can and can't do, the options and opportunities we see for ourselves, and how others will likely perceive us.

Your personal collection of stories can lean towards either a more negative or positive side, depending on who you are and the combination of your natural tendencies, upbringing and work experiences. They help me understand your thinking and beliefs about yourself. Through this discovery process, I aim to shift these stories towards possibilities, abundance, positivity and growth. I examine how you tell your career story when I listen to and read these stories to see whether it is a limiting, or an empowering, story.

What are limiting and empowering career stories? Both tell me the types of thoughts and beliefs that you hold about your career, yourself, your capabilities and what you think is possible for you:

- Limiting stories: The thoughts and beliefs expressed are those that place a limit on what you can do in your life. They do not allow you to reach your true potential and prevent you from achieving your purpose.

- Empowering stories: The thoughts and beliefs expressed empower you to achieve what you want in your career. They give you the confidence to succeed and search for opportunities for growth and improvement.

After categorizing your story as either 'limiting' or 'empowering', the next step is to peel the onion on your thoughts and beliefs so that we can reframe them to unlock your full potential. I often hear or read several limiting beliefs in these stories that impede growth, learning, decision-making and career plans.

CASE STUDY: Denise

Denise, a young professional, came to me for help. I asked her to state her career story in her words. She told me she had a good career thus far, five years into it. She received good performance feedback each year, but felt stuck, not growing and unhappy. She was very emotional while telling her story. She did not know what was next for her. Her bosses were not giving her feedback that helped her grow and she had tried applying for a few jobs with other companies but the response was not great. Her personal life could have been better. Although Denise felt that she knew a lot about her work, everyone thought that she was too young, so she felt that her voice needed to be more invited and heard in important matters. The external recruiters were telling her that she needed to be more experienced.

After our 'peeling the onion' discussion, we first identified and focused on her biggest limiting belief: 'Everyone thinks I am too young.' Because Denise believed everyone thought she was too young, she was hesitant to speak in meetings, was not assertive and put limits on expressing herself on critical issues. Our reframing on this limiting belief was around helping her focus on the value she brought to the discussion versus how people would think of her and her contributions because of her age or perceived lack of experience.

In some instances, to help professionals understand their stories better, I give them the task of writing down the following about each job in their career:

1. What was the primary reason you accepted a job?
2. What was the primary reason you left every job?
3. What would people say about you in each job?

Through this exercise, I am asking you to identify patterns. Your career decisions and choices give us further data points regarding your story and who you are. Whether you know it or not, you tell yourself stories about who you are, what you are capable of and how others perceive you on a daily basis. These internal stories shape the reality you experience, and you will find that you operate within their confines. Your story, whether limiting or empowering, also impacts the options and opportunities you perceive in your life.

My goal in this part of knowing yourself is for you to consciously examine your inner story and then reshape your narrative to create a more empowering reality. By consciously choosing an empowering story, you can break free of your limiting beliefs and unlock your true potential

What is your career story?

Career compass: Finding your 'true north' in direction and drive

Your stories also reveal how aware you are of what you want in your career, and why. As was the case of the high-potential leader who wanted to become a CEO, most often, people define very narrow or vague career aspirations and need clarification on their 'why'. Why do I want to become a CEO? What will that do for me?

The most important part of developing an empowering career story is to explore and determine where you are headed and what motivates you to go there by delving deep into your aspirations, motivations and objectives. It's crucial to take the time to explore and gain clarity on where you're headed, both in the short- and long-term, and what drives you to strive towards those goals.

Developing a clear sense of purpose and direction can provide a powerful sense of focus and motivation, helping you to stay on track and overcome any obstacles that may arise along the way. By understanding what truly drives you, you can build a career that aligns with your values and passions and, ultimately, achieve your desired fulfillment and success. Not being clear about your career direction and motivation is a significant barrier to unlocking your full potential.

If you have this clarity, you will have alignment between the outcome you desire and the activity that leads you there. The outcome here being a bigger or higher purpose you want from your career, and the activity being the steps or decisions you are taking in your career, ie, getting the next job you want or new skills you want to learn. Many professionals don't have clarity, or seek clarity, about their outcome and end up busily undertaking a lot of activity without making much progress.

Given the increased career options and opportunities now available, the length of careers and the number of jobs and companies that you will likely work for in your career, it is critical that you understand what outcome you want from your career or life and then align your activities to enable that outcome.

The best way to think about career direction and motivation is to reflect on two things: career success and fulfillment. Both are moving targets, meaning at different stages of your career and life they may change and evolve.

- Success is everything outside of you (extrinsic), like income goals, a car, house, finances, etc.

- Fulfillment means how you feel inside (intrinsic), like joy, happiness, making a difference in the world, helping others and having a higher-level purpose.

When people ask for my help in making career decisions, choices and progress, I ask them to write down what career success and fulfillment look like to them. There is no judgment on my part on what people write. I do not suggest fulfillment over success or vice versa.

Both are important and must be deeply personal and meaningful to you. With so much change and a heavy dose of introspection on what is important to us post-Covid-19, career success or fulfillment is not 'one size fits all'. It never was. Being clear about your career success and fulfillment puts you in the driving seat of your career.

If I look back at my career, the more focused I became on fulfillment, the more success followed. In the chart below, I have tried to capture what success and fulfillment have meant to me at various points in my career.

My career	Success	Fulfillment
Initial 5-7 years	Pay bills, enjoy some luxuries	Fueled by fear of failure, non-dependency on parents, learning
10-15 years	Savings, travel abroad, finer things in life, house, cars, college fund	Fueled by progression, diverse opportunities, growth, learning
Next 10-12 years	Enjoy luxuries, no loans, achieve financial freedom	Fueled by impact at work and outside of work, learning
Now	Able to leave my job	Fueled by inspiring others to succeed, learning

Depending on where you are with your career, you need to determine what success and fulfillment means to you. It does not have to be perfectly written; it must resonate with you. And it will keep changing over time.

Once you determine what success and fulfillment mean to you, you are in a great position to make career decisions. Each decision and action you take should help you get closer to your success and fulfillment. The key is alignment between your outcomes and actions. What does career success and fulfillment look like for you right now? Here are a few examples to get you started.

Career success

- Advancement and recognition: Promotions, awards, a high-ranking position, a prestigious title and high compensation.
- Financial stability and independence: Achieving financial security through your career. A comfortable lifestyle, financial freedom and the ability to support your desired lifestyle without financial stress.
- Work-life balance: Quality time for family, hobbies and self-care.
- Entrepreneurial success: A successful business or startup which has grown and thrived over time. Financial success, creation of employment opportunities and bringing innovative solutions to the market.

Career fulfillment

- Alignment with personal values: Career in alignment with core values and beliefs. Finding meaning and purpose in work, making a positive impact in areas you deeply care about.

- Helping others: Deriving fulfillment from helping and making a difference in the lives of others through your career and skills.

- Autonomy and creativity: Freedom to exercise creativity and autonomy in your career. Opportunity to innovate, think critically and make decisions independently, leading to a sense of fulfillment and accomplishment.

- Work that challenges and engages: Work that challenges you intellectually, provides ongoing learning opportunities and allows you to grow. Thriving in an environment that encourages your professional development and personal growth.

Inner kaleidoscope: Discovering the multifaceted aspects of yourself in career exploration

This is our third element. At work, you do not show up as just an employee. You are a complete person – someone's child and/or grandchild, perhaps a parent or a sibling. As you continue on your personal and professional journeys, it's important to reflect upon your whole self and all aspects of your life. You don't make career decisions in isolation.

As you think about what success and fulfillment mean to you, you need to look at yourself as a whole and reflect upon various areas of your life. When I first started to reflect on the different areas of my life together with my career, I started writing goals for different areas of my life:

1. Career: Become the Head of HR of a company.
2. Financial: Financial freedom by the age of fifty-five.
3. Health: Get off all prescription medications and lose weight.
4. Family: Be a great husband, father, son and sibling.
5. Fun: Play golf regularly, watch movies and meet friends regularly.
6. Participate in meaningful charity work.

I was delighted with them. Then I asked myself a question. How much time had I spent being great in each area in the last week or month? I realized that I didn't have the time to do all of my goals at a consistently great level. This was a crucial lesson for me. I had written all these ambitious goals in each area of my life, but I needed a realistic way to achieve them because of how I spent my time. Had I not asked the question regarding how much time I spent in each area, I would have let the goals stand as is and reviewed them sometime later only to be disappointed and unhappy. I had to make choices.

I now use the categories listed below to help me think. At different points in your life and career, certain categories will become more critical than others, and your definition of success and fulfillment may reflect that.

As an exercise, on a scale of 1–10 (1 being the worst and 10 being the best), score your current satisfaction levels against each category, and then think about where those scores should be ideally:

1. **Business/career:** Is your career where you want it to be?

2. **Finances:** Are you satisfied with your current earnings? Are you saving and/or investing what you would hope to be?

3. **Health:** How physically healthy are you? Are you satisfied with your level of fitness?

4. **Family and friends:** Can you spend the time you feel is necessary with your family and friends?

5. **Romance:** Are you spending the necessary quality time with your significant other?

6. **Personal growth:** How focused are you on personal growth? Are you satisfied with your direction?

7. **Fun and recreation:** Are you enjoying your life and making it fun? Are you satisfied with the level of activity that you do?

8. **Physical environment:** How satisfied are you with your contribution to society? Are you happy with your surroundings?

Completing this exercise is essential because it will help you make better career decisions. Not knowing where you stand viz-a-viz the whole self, you may make career decisions that do not align with your career success, fulfillment or both. Once you finish this exercise, revisit what you wrote under your career success and fulfillment statements and see if you want to refine those statements.

It's important to note that certain parts of your life will take a back seat at different points in time, and that's OK. By understanding your whole self, you can make sensible career decisions, set meaningful and realistic goals, create a career path that reflects your authentic identity and involve and inform others who are important in your life in your career plans, leading to a more fulfilling and rewarding career.

Core compass: Discovering your guiding values

Identifying and understanding your values is the fourth element and last part of knowing yourself and where you stand. Personal values are the behaviors and characteristics that are important to you, inspire you and help you make decisions. They reflect your deeply held convictions about what is important to you in life and work.

Knowing your values is very important to making good career decisions. Your values serve as a compass, providing clarity, purpose and a moral framework for building an exceptional career. When your values align with your work, you experience a sense of purpose and fulfillment. For example, if you value creativity and innovation, you may seek careers allowing you to express your creative ideas. If you value social impact, you might gravitate towards jobs in the non-profit sector or socially responsible companies. This alignment enables coherence and authenticity that can lead to greater success and personal satisfaction.

Today's world of work demands greater awareness of ethics in a much broader sense, and ethical decision-making is a critical skill. Your core guiding values also serve as a moral compass in an increasingly turbulent, complex and challenging work landscape. Think of your core values as a critical and essential asset for building an exceptional career.

An important lesson I learned during my career is that living my guiding values has fostered authentic connections with others who share similar values, leading to meaningful professional relationships, sponsorships, mentorships and collaborations. Looking back at my nineteen years at the Gillette Company (which later became P&G), I know I was in the right place to grow, develop and be recognized because many of my colleagues and leaders shared the same values. I did not select Gillette as a workplace because of my values, but I most certainly stayed for nineteen years because of them. To this day, my connections from Gillette are an essential part of my work and life.

Identifying your core guiding values will anchor you during times of change, providing an excellent foundation amid uncertainty and helping you make informed choices about the direction you want to take in your career. Today, choices are abundant and the pace of change is rapid; a robust set of values will guide your decisions, relationships and overall sense of purpose. You must reflect deeply in identifying what values are important to you. You can use the next two exercises to identify your guiding values.

Exercise 1: Reflect on peak experiences

Recall moments in your life in general, and career in particular, when you felt most fulfilled, satisfied or proud. Write down the details of these experiences, including what made them meaningful. Analyze the common themes, values and principles that emerge from these peak moments. If you take every job that you have held and write down your highs and lows for each, you will start to identify patterns, and these will help you identify your values. For example, all of my career highs had three consistent characteristics:

- I felt empowered.
- I was learning a ton.
- Innovation was an essential part of my job.

(Similarly, my lows also had consistent characteristics: a lack of trust and boredom with work.)

Exercise 2: Identify influential people

Think about individuals who have significantly impacted your life. These could be role models, mentors or people you admire. Consider the qualities, values and attributes you appreciate most about them. Reflect on why these qualities resonate with you and how they align with your aspirations. For example:

- Martin Luther King Jr (1929–1968): Deeply held personal values of equality, justice and non-violence. Martin Luther King's values were rooted in his faith and influenced his leadership style and strategies.[14]

- Mother Teresa (1910–1997): Deeply held personal values of compassion, service and empathy. Mother Teresa's values guided her tireless efforts

---

14 ML King, *The Autobiography of Martin Luther King, Jr* (Abacus Book, 6 April 2000)

to alleviate poverty and bring comfort to those in need.[15]

- Mahatma Gandhi (1869–1948): Deeply held personal values of truth, simplicity and self-discipline. These deeply held personal values guided Mahatma Gandhi's philosophy of life and influenced his approach to non-violent resistance and political activism.[16]

Common core values

Additionally, the list below describes some common core values to help you identify your own. It is not exhaustive and it is important to remember that you may have additional or different core values based on your unique circumstances and personal beliefs:

- **Integrity:** Acting with honesty, transparency and ethical principles.
- **Accountability:** Taking responsibility for one's actions, decisions and outcomes.
- **Excellence:** Striving for high quality, continuous improvement and exceptional work.
- **Respect:** Treating others with fairness, dignity and consideration.

---

15 B Kolodiejchuk, *Mother Teresa: Come Be My Light: The Private Writings of the Saint of Calcutta* (Rider, 7 August 2008)
16 L Fischer, *The Essential Gandhi: An Anthology of His Writings on His Life, Work, and Ideas* (Vintage Books, 12 November 2002)

- **Collaboration:** Working well with others, fostering teamwork and valuing diverse perspectives.

- **Innovation:** Embracing creativity, new ideas and finding innovative solutions.

- **Professionalism:** Demonstrating professionalism through behavior, appearance and a strong work ethic.

- **Leadership:** Taking initiative, inspiring others and guiding teams toward success.

- **Continuous learning:** Valuing personal and professional growth, seeking knowledge and adapting to change.

- **Work-life balance:** Prioritizing a healthy integration of work and personal life.

- **Customer focus:** Putting customers' needs and satisfaction at the forefront.

- **Empathy:** Understanding and considering others' emotions, perspectives and needs.

- **Social responsibility:** Contributing to the community and environment and making a positive impact.

- **Adaptability:** Being flexible and open to change and adjusting to new circumstances.

- **Autonomy:** Having the freedom and independence to make decisions and own one's work.

- **Growth mindset:** Embracing challenges, seeing failures as opportunities for growth and maintaining a positive outlook.
- **Balance:** Striving for balance and harmony across different aspects of life.
- **Trust:** Building trust through reliability, confidentiality and keeping commitments.
- **Diversity and inclusion:** Valuing and respecting diverse backgrounds, perspectives and experiences.
- **Service orientation:** A focus on serving others, whether clients, customers or the larger community.

Summary

It is very important that you spend enough time understanding yourself. In this chapter, I have shared with you the four most important elements of knowing yourself:

1. The power within: Unraveling your career story.
2. Career compass: Finding your 'true north' in direction and drive.
3. Inner kaleidoscope: Discovering the multifaceted aspects of yourself in career exploration.
4. Core compass: Discovering your guiding values.

By working on each of these elements, you will be able to identify where you stand today and where you want to head. You can effectively and efficiently plan for moving forwards to get to wherever you want to go, be it Boston, Toronto, Tokyo or Warsaw.

As we move into the next chapter, you will discover the strategies you need to adopt and deploy throughout your career to thrive by building upon the foundations of knowing yourself.

THREE
Strategies To Bulletproof Your Career

What is your secret sauce for building an extraordinary career? It's relevance (see Chapter 1). How do you begin this career journey/plan? By knowing yourself in-depth (see Chapter 2). In this chapter, I want to share the four most critical strategies you need to bulletproof your career. By bulletproof, I mean strategies you need to thrive in any career, at any stage, and against a continuously changing world of work.

Being an HR professional, I have had the opportunity to build talent strategies and programs, coached hundreds of professionals and observed successful (and not-so-successful) careers across the globe. Over time, I identified four key strategies that differentiate successful and unsuccessful careers. My career has benefited immensely from them. The strategies are:

1. Futureproof your career: Embrace lifelong *learning* for lasting relevance.
2. Career by design: *Proactively* craft your path to success.
3. Follow your 'north star': Let your *aspiration* guide your career journey.
4. Multiply your opportunities: Harness the *networking* advantage for career growth.

Futureproof your career: Embrace lifelong learning for lasting relevance

Learning is a self-investment that you must make. You cannot afford not to. In my training programs on taking charge of careers and career coaching sessions, I start this section of our discussion by asking everyone, 'What is your learning strategy?' I rarely get a robust answer. Most people don't have a strategy or know their preferred learning method. This leads to learning not being a habit for them, and they find it hard to blend it into their lives. It then becomes a chore and they find it immensely difficult to find time to learn. Life gets in the way. So, how do you learn? What is your learning strategy?

To remain relevant, adapt and thrive in this ever-changing world of work, you need to learn continuously and develop yourself. You need a personal learning strategy that allows you to seek new and relevant knowledge, skills, experience and education. Whatever your strategy, elements of it must seamlessly blend into your daily/weekly routine, not as an added chore or task. This learning is often self-taught, voluntary and focused on an area that improves your career or life. Here are some steps that need to be included in your learning strategy:

- **Assess your current skills and knowledge.** You do this by identifying areas where you excel and those that may require improvement or acquisition. For example, if you're currently at manager level and your next career goal is to become a director, what skills and knowledge do you excel at, and what do you need? Link this learning to your career aspirations and goals. This assessment will serve as a starting point for your learning journey.

- **Establish learning goals for each year.** Just as you develop and pursue performance goals, you need to establish learning goals that align with your career aspirations.

- **Keep yourself informed and updated on your industry's latest trends and developments.** Subscribe to relevant newsletters, industry publications and online communities. Follow experts, thought leaders, influencers and companies on social media platforms. Attend conferences, seminars, podcasts, and webinars to gain insights into emerging technologies, practices and opportunities.

- **Seek diverse learning opportunities.** These should include online courses and certifications, workshops, training programs, mentorship, coaching, new experiences at work, peer discussions, books and more. Over time you will discover what kind of learning works best for you.

- **Allocate time on your calendar to learning.** It's not going to happen otherwise.

- **Apply and share your knowledge.** Seek opportunities within your current role or through side projects to apply the skills you've learned. So many people attend training programs and other learning sessions but do not apply their new knowledge to their work.

- **Be open to learning.** Explore new technologies, methodologies and approaches.

Let me share a few learning strategies that have worked for me. I read relevant material on the internet nearly every day for 5–10 minutes and then share it with as many connections as I think will benefit from it. These can be articles, quotes, book recommendations, documents, etc. Over time, I've figured out where I will seek knowledge from (for example, I enjoy reading *Harvard Business Review* articles or LinkedIn content), increased my reading speed and found a way to engage with my connections. I tell them that they have no obligation to respond, but someone quite often does. These exchanges are brief, but help me store the information in my brain. This strategy helps me master topics, learn quickly, and share and engage with others. It helps me connect the dots rapidly where others might see ambiguity. I have been doing this for over twenty years and it's a habit. After every project, initiative or role, I also pause and reflect on what I have learned about myself. This helps me focus on what I do well, where I need to learn more, and where I made mistakes. This expands my brain storage, helps my brain to understand and read patterns, and enhances my learning of the subject.

Whatever your learning strategy, here is how to approach it:

1. Understand how, and where, you seek your information and knowledge. It should be trusted, reliable and accurate. There is a lot of information available everywhere. Find the source of the information.

2. Understand how you make sense of the information and knowledge. Reflect on how you will use and personalize it.

3. Understand how you will share it. It should enhance your own learning, help others learn and lead to collaboration.

4. Blend it into your routine and make it a habit.

5. Most importantly, make it relevant to what your career aspiration or goals are.

Career by design: Proactively craft your path to success

In August 2001, I was based in Moscow, Russia, as the HR Director for the Gillette Company when I received an important call from the president of the region in London, our regional headquarters. He told me that he would like me to be the HR Director of the region (numerous countries covering Eastern Europe, Africa and the Middle East) based in London. I was ecstatic. I could not imagine a better role for myself. My wife was also delighted, as she had grown up in London. Everything was perfect. Over the next few weeks, many people unofficially knew about my promotion, and my wife started thinking about where we would live and which schools the children would attend.

Then 9/11 happened, shocking the entire world. Two weeks after the tragedy, the president called and apologized. I would not be getting the job in London. Internal moves in other regions were not taking place and the incumbent in London could not move, so I could not replace him. I was devastated, and so was my wife. Many years later, I still feel the pain, but the incident taught me one of the greatest lessons in my career. After a few days of reflection, what I learned propelled me to success I had never imagined for myself.

On reflection, I realized that because I'd had a very successful career at the Gillette Company, I had given much of the control of my career growth to them. I was being promoted regularly, moving geographies and performing well. As a result, when I did not get the London job, I had no clue what my next job would be. It was not a good feeling. I realized that I was being reactive rather than proactive. Within a few months of the incident, I received offers from the company regarding other jobs. I politely declined the first two offers. They were good, but I didn't want the company to offer me roles because they felt sorry for me or roles that would just take me out of Russia. I wanted them to give me a role with equal or greater impact and influence than the London job. Finally, nine months later, I accepted an excellent role in Boston that changed my career trajectory completely.

I could have positioned myself as a victim of circumstances following 9/11. My friends told me not to decline the jobs the company was offering. But I had figured out what proactivity meant for my career. I did not control the circumstances, but I did own my response to them. I took charge of what I wanted, did not let my performance suffer, and did not let my attitude or demeanor fall. I recognized that the company felt terrible and wanted to do something and I leveraged that. From then onwards, I was proactive in shaping my career. I took control of what, and where, my next role would be and stood steadfast until I got it. It wasn't the title, or that it was in Boston; it was about finding the right impact and influence in a role. It was exhilarating!

In Stephen Covey's book *The 7 Habits of Highly Effective People*,[17] the first habit is being proactive. Reactive people cast themselves as victims of circumstances and spend too much time thinking about things they do not control directly and very little time on the things they can control, but proactive people take action on the things they control or can influence.

Who is responsible for your career? I also ask everyone this question. Is it not *your* career? Most often, people wait for their company or boss to do something to move them forwards and do not take responsibility for their own careers. They adopt a reactive mode. If you don't do much about your career, then why should someone else? Given the changes in the world of work and the demise of the predefined steps in the career ladder, you must be proactive in shaping your career. Don't wait for your boss or company to do something about it. It's your career. Take control.

In my example above, I could have considered myself an indirect victim of circumstances in losing my dream job. Had I done that, I would have let the events lead me to a not-so-great job, and who knows where that would have taken my career. I took responsibility for the next step in my career regarding what I wanted and influenced the company to think of better opportunities for me. It led me to be much more proactive

---

17   S Covey, *The 7 Habits of Highly Effective People* (Free Press, 1 January 1988)

about my career after that situation and served me exceptionally well. Three things have helped me:

1. I prepare myself for whatever is next. I think about the next steps and use a development plan to act on them. I leverage my strengths to drive my career progress.
2. I seek feedback from a variety of sources. Receiving feedback tells me where I am right now versus where I want to be.
3. Importantly, I deliver above-average performance.

Creating your path to career success and fulfillment means always taking ownership of your career and not delegating the ownership to anyone else. It also means continuously improving on the things you do control in your career and not wasting time on things you do not control. Put yourself in charge. These are some examples of the things that you do control regarding your career: mindset, attitude, learning, performance, ambition, courage, relationships, collaboration, seeking meaningful feedback. What else can you think of that you control?

Follow your 'north star': Let your aspiration guide your career journey

If you want an extraordinary career of success and fulfillment, you must follow your aspiration. Yes, aspirations may change and evolve over time, but you must know what you aspire to before you can pursue it.

John was about to be let go from his CEO job when he contacted me and asked to be connected to executives and headhunters I knew. I asked him what his career aspiration was. He gave me a decent answer, but it was clear that he had not given it much thought. Wanting or taking a job without understanding where we want our careers to head is common. The result is that most people are generally unhappy with their jobs or careers. Not knowing your aspiration is like getting into a rudderless boat. Aspiration lies at the intersection of talent, passion and other people's needs.

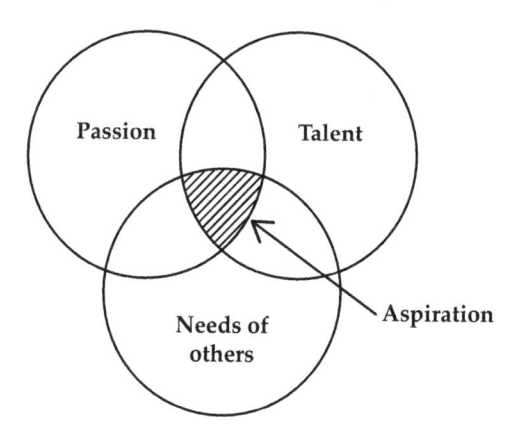

John and I spent considerable time discussing his talent, what he is passionate about and whether there is a need in the market for that. Finding your own aspiration requires an honest and thorough self-exploration and understanding of what you value, your strengths and what you enjoy and are energized by. Once you determine this, it will become abundantly clear what kind of jobs will enable you to move towards your aspiration. Three things have worked for me:

1. I keep refining my aspiration. I learned not to wait until I have the perfectly worded aspiration. Just write something now, work on it and it will start coming to you.
2. Once I write my aspiration, then I have an action plan that lists the milestones I need to achieve in the short- and long-term. Micro- and macro-wins.
3. I share my aspiration with others constantly. This reinforces my aspiration and keeps me honest. The magic happens when I see that it lights a spark in someone else.

Adding these three ingredients to your career will greatly enhance your chances of success. We will talk more about this later in the book when we discuss writing your career plan.

Multiply your opportunities: Harness the networking advantage for career growth

In 2010 I was working for Dun & Bradstreet, based in New Jersey, as VP of HR International. I received a message from a former Gillette Pakistan colleague,

Uzma Mirza. It was a pleasant surprise. I had hired her for the HR function at Gillette Pakistan in 1996. I left for Gillette's World Headquarters in Boston a few months later, but Uzma had already created a good impression on me through her performance, learning agility and attitude. We were now connecting after a gap of fourteen years. Uzma told me she was also living in New Jersey and working on a contract as a Total Rewards consultant in New York. By coincidence, my company was also looking for a Total Rewards professional. I referred Uzma to our company VP of Total Rewards. Uzma was interviewed and got the job. What's the point in sharing this with you? Uzma is a good example of the multiplier impact of networking:

- She has continuously built and expanded her network throughout her career. This has created job opportunities for her and allowed her to determine the lifestyle she wants. She has done this through her performance, attitude and relationship-building.

- She and I worked together for only a few months, but fourteen years later, I still remembered her capabilities and attitude, and she took the initiative to reach out to her network. Once she joined Dun & Bradstreet, she further expanded her network in the Total Rewards space, leading her to several more opportunities.

- She has now built up a robust network in the Total Rewards space and is sought for her experience and skills. She can take breaks when she feels appropriate, knowing that she has built up a strong network where opportunities for her abound.

In the earlier chapters, we discussed how the world of work is changing and that, on average, you are going to work for twelve or more companies in your career. You will also need to unlearn and relearn skills and knowledge. Part of this means that you will have to look at networking in a new way. You will need a networking strategy for yourself.

Networking is no longer about contacting your connections when you need a job or are considering a change. You need to continuously build your network. The stronger your network, the better you will be able to navigate change in the workplace. By building a solid network, you can create opportunities for yourself. Most people reach out to their connections when they need a job without having nurtured those connections over time. The result is often that those connections can't help, and you may feel let down. If you are intentionally building and nurturing your network, it is more likely that you will get access to the hidden job market – jobs that are not advertised or posted – and you will find that opportunities will find you versus you finding opportunities.

At work, we create impressions of ourselves with people around us. These impressions are a great starting point for building networks. Many of these colleagues are going to work somewhere else in time. You need to view everyone at work as a potential addition to your network. I have plotted my career journey in the chart below, from my MBA to where I am now. At each step, I created an impression on the people I studied or worked with, consciously or unconsciously. Somewhere along the way, I realized I needed to intentionally nurture these connections as my network. It paid off well. My first break as a Head of HR of a company came through a connection I made as a trainee in Boston eighteen years earlier, and the two biggest jobs I have had in my career have come through the network I intentionally nurtured.

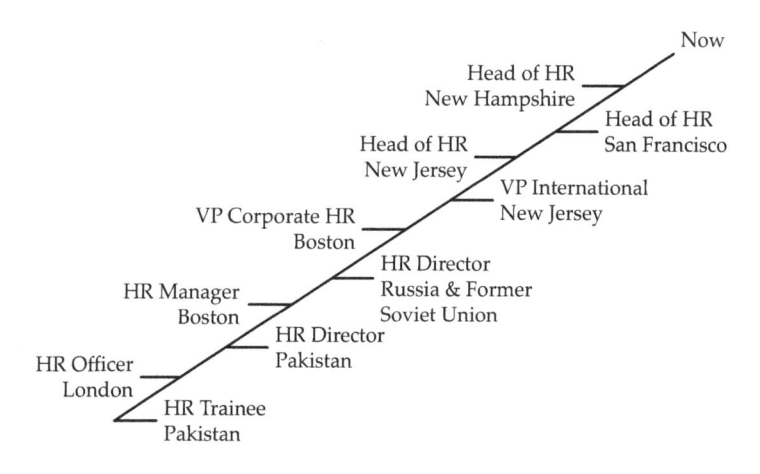

```
                                                              Now
                                    Head of HR
                                    New Hampshire
                                                    Head of HR
                            Head of HR              San Francisco
                            New Jersey
                                            VP International
            VP Corporate HR                 New Jersey
                    Boston
                                HR Director
        HR Manager              Russia & Former
            Boston              Soviet Union
                        HR Director
HR Officer              Pakistan
    London
            HR Trainee
            Pakistan
```

Networking today is about more than just finding jobs. It is also about gaining knowledge, learning new skills and seeing and anticipating changes. When you work in a company, you are usually focused on the work and challenges your company faces. But you must find time to look outside your company and build broader connections in your industry and profession. For example, if you nurture a LinkedIn 'thought leadership' network, you will learn new perspectives and likely see where businesses and occupations are headed, given the challenges.

Over the years, I have built three kinds of networks. Your own networks should be evaluated depending on where you are in your career and what your current aspirations are:

1. The first network concerns future jobs that you are interested in or might need to consider. (Ask yourself: What is my next likely job? Who do I have in my network that can help me identify future opportunities?)

2. The second is your knowledge and learning network. (Ask yourself: What do I need to learn and know more about? Who do I have in my network who can help me with this?)

3. The third is your network of people you want to advise, coach or mentor. (Ask yourself: What can I help others with in my profession or industry? Who do I have in my network that I can help?)

Summary

This chapter has examined four essential career strategies for success in the modern world. I have observed these in many successful careers across the globe and have used these strategies to drive success for myself. By embracing lifelong learning, proactively crafting your career path, following your aspirations and harnessing the power of networking, you can position yourself for lasting relevance and fulfillment in an ever-changing work environment. The one common theme that these four strategies have is they are career-long approaches; they are not 'one and done' tactics.

As you reflect on and embrace these strategies, remember that the key to success lies in the strategies themselves and your willingness to embrace them and take action. Embracing and acting on these strategies puts the future of your career squarely in your hands.

FOUR
Mindset For Career Success

Cristiano Ronaldo, arguably one of the best soccer players in history, was asked what he thinks differentiates him from so many other soccer players in the world? He replied that his biggest strength is his 'mind', as talent alone is not enough. He believes his mindset allows him to make great decisions daily, particularly when things are not going his way. His mindset drives him to work hard and continue to learn and grow. He attributes this mindset to his sustained success at the highest level of soccer.

Contrast that with hundreds of people I have met in my career in Human Resources across the world who are on autopilot and sleepwalking in their careers. They have career dreams and ambitions, but they do nothing about them because they let negative thoughts of failure, doubt, safety, timing and bad luck fill their heads and end up doing nothing. They are usually stuck in the same job for years with no foreseeable career progression. They may have had bad experiences, or someone might have taught them these negative beliefs, which are then lodged deep in their minds. They let their minds control them through a default setting that stops them from taking the initiative or ownership of actions instead of choosing to control their minds.

Please do not get me wrong; not all triggers of the mind are negative. Many triggers are positive, and we need them. The trick is understanding how different situations and stimuli trigger your mindset and how to alter them for the best results. In Ronaldo's example, he has trained his mind and controls it to get the desired results. His ambition has been to be the best soccer player in history. To become that, he needs to 1) be disciplined in his life, 2) train consistently, 3) improve constantly, and 4) make several smart choices daily. Instead of letting his mind operate in a default mode, he has trained his mind to be strong and push him towards success. Success for him is not an event. It is a daily process.

Is your mind operating in a default mode? Are you training and controlling your mind to get the career results you desire? In this chapter, I would like to share how your mindset is critical to your career success. Having observed hundreds of professionals and leaders across the world, I know the ability to control your mindset has been the most significant differentiator between those who have had sustainable career success and those who have fallen short. It is definitely a skill that you can, and must, learn if you want sustainable career success.

Your 'mindset' is your set of mental inclinations, attitudes or beliefs. It shapes how you see the world and yourself. Everything you do, feel and experience is shaped by your beliefs and attitudes, hence, your mindset, so this is critical to your success or failure. Your beliefs and attitudes are formed by what you experience, what you are taught by others, and what you teach yourself. You then act, behave and think based on these beliefs and attitudes. For example, if a child experiences trauma because of a parent's alcoholism, that child might have a belief that alcohol is terrible and may then act and behave according to that belief.

The four critical mindset types

There are four types of mindsets that are critical to sustainable career success:

1. Growth mindset

2. Abundance mindset

3. Feedback mindset

4. Inner-validation mindset

Growth mindset

The terms 'growth mindset' and 'fixed mindset' were first coined by Stanford psychologist Caroline Dweck in her book *Mindset: The New Psychology of Success*.[18] According to Dweck, a growth mindset is one where you believe that your talents are not fixed. They can be changed and are constantly being developed. Your learning does not stop once you leave school, college or any learning institute, you are continuously learning new knowledge and skills, whether at work or elsewhere. You are also not afraid of failing as you recognize that this is also a learning experience. A fixed mindset, on the other hand, is one where you believe your intelligence is set. You either have it, or you don't. Fixed mindsets have the tendency to go where the least resistance is expected. Do you have a fixed or growth mindset? The short exercise below will give you an initial idea. Go through the statements below and decide which ones you agree most with:

1. I am capable of changing myself.

2. People either have a specific talent or they don't. They can't just acquire talent for things in life.

3. I came into this world with a certain amount of intelligence, and I cannot change that.

---

18   CS Dweck, *Mindset: The New Psychology of Success* (Ballantine Books, 1 January 2013)

4. It does not matter who you are, there is little you can do to improve your basic abilities and personality.

5. I can learn new things and improve my intelligence.

6. I can develop new talents and skills by learning, studying, working hard and applying new skills.

Agreeing more with statements 1, 5, and 6 indicates a growth mindset, and agreeing more with statements 2, 3 and 4 indicates a fixed mindset.

Why is a growth mindset important? In Chapter 1, we discussed how the world of work is rapidly changing and will continue to do so. A growth mindset is critical to be relevant and thrive in this environment. I often hear professionals and leaders say that they have a growth mindset because they are open-minded and flexible, but they continue to rely on past processes and methods because these are successful. They are unwilling to learn or try new ideas, methods or techniques. They are constantly trying to prove that they are right. They actually have a fixed mindset. A growth mindset requires learning, unlearning and relearning to evolve and continuously improve.

When it comes to careers, the greatest threat to your success is trying to avoid failure. So many professionals focus on preventing failure and staying where they are in their careers for longer, but avoiding challenges and mistakes in today's world is like the ostrich burying its head in the sand. Executives who focus on learning from challenges and failures are better prepared for growth and more significant challenges and will be more successful in their careers.

In the early 2000s, the Gillette Company relaunched its high-potential development program. It engaged RHR International, a consulting firm, pioneers in organizational psychology specializing in executive development, talent management, and organizational effectiveness. As part of the project, the firm helped Gillette answer the question, 'What is the strongest predictor of high potential?' RHR's research into this question came back with a professional's 'learning ability' as the strongest predictor of their talent.[19]

In multiple scenarios, I have observed leaders fail to engage and motivate their teams because of their fixed mindset, which stifles growth and morale. Leaders often assume they need to know all the answers and feel insecure about challenging their thinking and ideas. In contrast, growth mindset leaders recognize that they cannot have all the answers and need to develop a team that brings different capabilities and ideas. They create an environment where diverse ideas are welcomed, and failure is a vital learning and development opportunity. If you have fixed

---

19 RHR International is a global leadership consulting firm specializing in executive development, talent management, and organizational effectiveness. They provide services to help organizations optimize their leadership capabilities and enhance overall performance.

mindset tendencies in today's world of work, it will likely contribute to stress and performance issues. More importantly, you will miss out on career growth opportunities. The future belongs to you if you have growth mindset tendencies.

Let's look at a few famous individuals to understand the two mindsets better. See if you agree with the characteristics below. It's important to remember that everyone can have a mix of fixed and growth mindset qualities in different parts of their lives or at various stages in their careers.

Fixed mindset examples

Henry Ford (1863–1947):

- Resistance to innovation: Ford was known for his resistance to adopting new technologies and designs, sticking to the Model T for an extended period despite changing market demands.

- Limited perspective on consumer preferences: Ford famously stated, 'Any customer can have a car painted any color that he wants, so long as it is black,' indicating a lack of openness to customization and individual customer preferences.

- Autocratic management style: Ford's management approach emphasized strict control and limited autonomy for employees, inhibiting opportunities for growth and creativity.[20]

Emperor Napoleon Bonaparte (1769–1821):

- Stubbornness: Napoleon was known for his stubbornness and reluctance to listen to advice or opinions that contradicted his own.

- Resistance to change: He was resistant to adapt his strategies and tactics, leading to setbacks in battles and military campaigns.

- Authoritarian leadership style: Napoleon's leadership style emphasized control and conformity, limiting input and collaboration from others.[21]

Growth mindset examples

Marie Curie (1867–1934):

- Determination and perseverance: Marie Curie's relentless dedication to her scientific research, despite facing numerous obstacles and gender-based discrimination, exemplified a growth mindset.

- Intellectual curiosity: She displayed an insatiable thirst for knowledge and a passion for discovery,

---

20 S Watts, *The People's Tycoon: Henry Ford and the American Century* (Vintage Books, 15 January 2007)
21 F McLynn, *Napoleon: A Biography* (Pimlico, 5 November 1998)

continually expanding her understanding of radiation and its properties.

- Commitment to education: Curie prioritized education and played an instrumental role in establishing scientific institutions, recognizing the importance of nurturing future generations of scientists.[22]

Amelia Earhart (1897–1937):

- Courage and risk-taking: Amelia Earhart's pioneering spirit and willingness to venture into uncharted territories showcased a growth mindset, as she pushed the boundaries of aviation and women's roles in society.

- Determination and resilience: Despite facing numerous challenges and setbacks, Earhart remained determined and resilient, demonstrating a belief in continuous improvement and learning from experiences.

- Advocacy for women's empowerment: Earhart's advocacy for gender equality and her efforts to inspire women to pursue their dreams highlighted her growth-oriented mindset and belief in the potential for personal and societal progress.[23]

---

22 E Curie, *Madame Curie: A Biography* (Style Press, 6 August 2007)
23 S Wels, *Amelia Earhart: The Thrill of It* (Running Press, 24 September 2009)

Abundance mindset

Opportunity knocks on every door in our careers. Early in my career, I stumbled into a situation that provided me with an outstanding mindset approach that I have hung on to, and shared with others at every opportunity. I was an HR Trainee at the Gillette Company world headquarters in Boston. It was an eighteen-month assignment as part of the company's award-winning International Trainee program. A few months into my assignment, I saw an object covered by a plastic cover on a table in my boss' office. I asked my boss what was underneath it, and he told me it was a computer for which he had no use. (It was 1990.) I asked him if I could have it, as I had learned a little about computers at my university and wanted to further my learning. My boss had no objections, so over the next few months, I started to learn more about the computer. I engaged with other trainees to teach me and for them to learn as well. I showed my boss that I could create pie charts, graphs and presentations.

A few months went by and then one afternoon at 4.30pm, I received a phone call from my boss to come to his office as he needed my help. He introduced me to a Director of HR (responsible for Africa, the Middle East and Eastern Europe) based in London, but visiting Boston for a very important presentation to the company's Chairman. The next day! My boss had hand-scribbled many changes on the presentation as part of prepping the HR Director. The presentation was over fifty pages. Since I was now very handy with graphs, charts and presentation slides, my boss wanted me to change the slides. There was no USB, CD or floppy disk containing the original presentation, so I had to literally recreate almost the entire thing. It was 4.30pm and they had a company dinner to go to, so my boss told me they would pick me up at 5am the following day so we could finish the document before the 9am presentation to the Chairman. I was excited and scared at the same time. Excited about the opportunity and scared because the Chairman was a very tough leader. He had a reputation for having impacted careers based on the presentations made to him.

As I walked back to my office, fear started to loom. I envisioned my boss and the HR Director breathing down my neck at 5am and me not knowing how to do something they wanted in the presentation. At that moment, I made a decision that was essentially aimed at saving my trainee job. I quickly went to my boss' office and told them that I would start working on the presentation that evening and do as much as I could, and then they could pick me up at 5am the following day.

I started work on the presentation at about 6pm (no laptops to take home) and finished the edits to the presentation at midnight. I was so relieved that I'd made an excellent decision to start working that evening. The following day, my boss picked me up at

5am. We reviewed the presentation, made a few more edits and finished it at 7.30am. Both thanked me profusely, but I was just relieved I hadn't screwed up. The presentation went smoothly and I moved on, forgetting all about it.

'Good story,' you may say, 'but what's the lesson?' Well, the story did not end there. About two months after helping the Director of HR from London, he spoke to my boss and said he wanted me to take up a position in the London office, working in his team. I was delighted and gleefully accepted. Not only was I going to an excellent assignment in London, but Amber (my now-wife), a girl I really liked, was in London. Being in a position to help both those leaders and then taking responsibility by starting that evening versus the following morning not only delivered the results they wanted, but created a great impression of who I was. Opportunity knocked, and I was ready.

The lesson I learned from this was that opportunity knocks on every door in our careers. When the opportunity knocks, it encounters three kinds of people:

- The first person does not hear the knock and is not ready for the opportunity. The opportunity goes a-begging.
- The second person hears the opportunity knock, but is not ready. Again, the opportunity goes a-begging.

- The third kind of person is one who not only hears the knock, but is also ready for the opportunity.

After this happy situation, I developed a mindset of hearing opportunities and being ready. Seeing my career progress, many of my friends and colleagues have often mentioned that I have been 'lucky'. Maybe I have. But I have also looked ahead, not knowing what exactly my next opportunity will be, but always working on improving myself and watching out for opportunities. This mindset has always made me feel ready for whatever comes next from a career perspective, opened my mind to many possibilities, and driven me to learn new things as I see them.

That day in Boston, I reacted to the opportunity in fear and put in the extra hours, and I was ready because I self-taught myself to prepare presentations. In today's challenging and changing work environment, opportunities will come your way, although they might be in disguise. Are you going to be ready?

Feedback mindset

Feedback is a gift. Looking back at my early career, I know I was driven by fear. I feared losing my job because I was not good enough. Over time, however, I learned to embrace feedback. It was a fundamental mindset change. How did that change occur?

The change started with my first official performance review below, which was not very flattering.

> Inform the various exposures the trainee should have in order to improve his professional development.
>
> Asad is intelligent, hardworking and honest.
>
> To be successful in Gillette and in Personnel he must improve his image, style and the way he presents himself. The areas that need immediate and significant change include: speaking up and with conviction, as well as being aggressive and direct.
>
> He also must demonstrate his motivation/interest in what he does and the company he does it for.

This feedback hit me like a ton of bricks. I thought I would be fired. After sitting on it for a few days, I realized it was really up to me to do something about it (Lesson #1). So, I mustered courage (Lesson #2), returned to my boss, and said, 'Thank you for the feedback, but what do I do with it'? I did not know it then, but my conversation created a constructive feedback environment between him and me (Lesson #3). Instead of fighting the feedback, I digested it and demonstrated that I could receive feedback constructively and work on it to improve myself.

MINDSET FOR CAREER SUCCESS

He recommended that I enlist in the Dale Carnegie 'Effective Communications & Public Speaking' training program. So, every Monday from 6pm–10pm, I attended this program at the Sheraton Hotel in Boston for fourteen weeks, joining fifty other participants from different companies. It was just what the doctor ordered for me because I felt they pushed me out of my comfort zone in each session. At the end of the program, I was chosen as the individual who'd improved the most and was awarded the prestigious Dale Carnegie pen. It felt great.

I showed it to my boss. You could have seen his smile from a hundred miles away. He was so proud. He shared the news and my progress with other senior leaders (Lesson #4) and often reinforced my progress with me (Lesson #5). I became much more confident about speaking with conviction, expressing my thoughts and demonstrating my passion. This experience was the start of my embracing feedback as my mindset changed from fear to realizing the benefits. Not every feedback conversation will be constructive, but you must learn to react constructively.

A feedback mindset centers not only on how individuals perceive and respond to feedback, but also on creating an environment for receiving feedback. In summary:

- Employees with a strong feedback mindset are open to receiving feedback, regardless of whether it's positive or constructive. They do not wait until a formal review takes place and they do not only get it from their boss. They look for multiple sources.

- They seek both positive and constructive feedback to understand how to leverage their strengths and where to make improvements.
- They are honest with themselves and are willing to acknowledge areas where they can improve.
- They act on the feedback and take ownership of their development.

Inner-validation mindset

Only you can determine your value. At work, we often don't know our own value. Instead, we give that responsibility to our bosses, peers and the company and wait for a performance review, salary increase, promotion or recognition to tell us our value. The company demonstrates how it values us through the job, title, compensation and recognition we receive. Our peers show us how they value us by including or excluding us in conversations, meetings and projects. Often, we gauge our value by comparing ourselves to others.

These are the characteristics necessary to develop an inner-validation mindset:

1. Set a standard in your mind and try to improve every day to get there. Ronaldo has set the bar

for being the world's best soccer player. He measures himself against that and knows what to do daily to be the best. I used to compare myself to other HR professionals, particularly my peers who were getting ahead in their careers. I often thought, 'Why them and not me?' With a lot of reflection, discussions with others and reading books, I realized that others cannot determine my value as well as I can, because I know myself better than them. This mindset shift in me led me to passionately pursue excellence in my field. I value feedback and opinions, but also attach a filter of honest self-reflection.

2. Trust your judgment to make informed decisions based on your knowledge and experience. Seek input from others, but ultimately, rely on your own judgment to guide your actions.

3. Be willing to step outside your comfort zone and take calculated risks that align with your goals and values.

4. Trust yourself to handle challenges and setbacks and view them as opportunities for learning and growth.

5. Build resilience to bounce back from failures and setbacks and be kind to yourself.

These characteristics do not appear automatically or overnight. You need to consciously and consistently practice them to develop an inner-validation mindset at work. The benefits to your career will be self-confidence, authenticity and personal growth. On the other hand, lacking an inner-validation mindset can lead to self-doubt, indecisiveness and fear of failure.

Summary

With a growth mindset, you are more likely to continuously improve your capability, adapt to changes and overcome career obstacles.

With an abundance mindset, you approach your career optimistically and seek new possibilities and collaborations.

With a feedback mindset, you seek feedback to enhance your performance, and use it as a tool for self-improvement and your development.

With an inner-validation mindset, you become more resilient, take calculated risks and prioritize personal wellbeing and career fulfillment.

These mindsets work together, sometimes overlapping, to fuel your sustainable career success and fulfillment. The trick is to make these mindset shifts happen and make your mind work for you, instead of allowing your mind to control you.

FIVE
Career-Building And Navigation Power Skills

Building an extraordinary career in turbulent times requires a potent and evolving combination of strategies, mindset, skills and actions. I have covered career strategies in Chapter 3 and career mindset in Chapter 4 and I will discuss actions (career plan steps) in Chapter 6. This chapter will explore the power skills required to build and navigate a successful career amid constant and fast change.

It is important to note two things as your read this chapter. First, when I say 'power skills', I refer to skills needed to construct and navigate an extraordinary career and not skills required to be a good leader or do a job well. Just as Lionel Messi manages his football career, plays in the Argentinian football team and is captain of the Argentinian team, they are all connected but distinct. Each requires different skills. Second, by skills, I specifically mean the learned power of building and navigating your entire career competently. In other words, developing an aptitude or ability to master your career over time.

Why do you need power skills?

Career-building and navigation power skills play a crucial role in enhancing your employability, impact and career growth, and most importantly, in achieving success and fulfillment in your career journey as determined by you.

These skills are a critical requirement now and in the future. The changing world of work and our own evolving set of expectations require self-management of our careers through these skills. Not having these skills will result in poor career self-management, leading to stagnation, limited skill development, reduced networking opportunities, decreased adaptability, diminished job satisfaction and a narrower range of career options. Taking an active role in your career management allows you to navigate changes, pursue growth opportunities and increase your chances of long-term success and fulfillment.

It will require knowing yourself and your life goals and making career decisions that fulfill your needs and the needs of the organization you work for. The skills I am recommending served me well in my career, helping me achieve the pinnacle of my chosen field. I want the same for you. Whether or not you reach your ultimate destination, these skills will give you the ability to make good decisions and make the career journey worthwhile.

Lacking career-building and navigation skills in a fast-changing world of work makes it easy to get lost in the chaos. I did that in the early stages of my career. I focused only on the changing environment around me, thinking that I would let the situation settle down and hoping for some divine intervention or just plain good luck. At other times, I was just in cruise control about my career, and then suddenly felt lost and unsure about what my next steps were as the world changed around me or, over time, realized that I no longer wanted the same things in my career that I once did. This mindset may have worked in the distant past when there was far less change, but not today. Are you equipped to make the best career decisions for yourself? Let's look at two scenarios to highlight the necessity of power skills.

1. **Shane** works for a terrific company. He's been with them for about twelve years and is performing well as per the feedback he has received. However, the company has had a few mass layoffs recently, leaving Shane wondering if the next one will have his name on the list. Most recently, the company has offered him and all other employees voluntary redundancy with

an average severance package. Without suitable career-building and navigation skills, he feels anxious about his decision. Should he take the voluntary redundancy package and find a job elsewhere, or not take it and risk being a victim of a potential next layoff?

2. **Mohammad** has worked with companies with great brands and has done well throughout his eighteen-year career. About three years ago, circumstances led him to work as a consultant for one of those companies. He took up the opportunity thinking he would work as a consultant for two or three years and then find a meaningful full-time job elsewhere. However, two situations have recently come up. The first is that Mohammad has become aware that his consulting assignment with his current company might end in the next six months or so. That is how he is reading the tea leaves. The second situation that has popped up is that, out of the blue, a company in a different industry saw his profile on LinkedIn and have offered him a job. The job is different from what he has done in the past, a different industry, he knows no one in that company, it requires a significant lifestyle change and offers less pay than he is making as a consultant. Mohammad feels very anxious about his decision. Does he take the offer from the other company and secure a longer-term compensation, or wait until his consulting assignment finishes?

In both these situations, the lack of career-building and navigation skills cause them anxiety and can lead them to make sub-optimal career decisions through defensive and survival-focused decisions. Shane was inclined to take the voluntary severance package, thinking more layoffs may come and he may not receive the same package if he is picked, but not being clear about what was next for him or understanding his future job landscape. Mohammad had become comfortable with his existing compensation and lifestyle and was in cruise control mode, not thinking beyond the current scenario.

What did they end up doing? First, both reached out to me for advice. I would highly recommend you reaching out to someone knowledgeable to seek advice, whether or not you have the career-building and navigation power skills. In the case of Shane, after a meaningful discussion, he realized that he had not planned for what and where his next job would be if took the voluntary severance package. He felt more comfortable staying with the company, performing at a high level and working out a plan for what he might do if he is laid off in the future. After a series of discussions with Mohammad, he decided not to accept the new job offer, as spending time with his young daughter was very important for him. He, too, has started working on a plan to secure a meaningful job before a possible end of his consulting assignment.

Do you perhaps face a similar situation or have a tough career decision on the horizon? The chances of you facing changes like these and many others in your work environment are growing exponentially. The pace of change in careers and career opportunities has been accelerating in recent years due to a variety of factors, including technological advancements, globalization, changing consumer preferences and changing employee expectations of the workforce. According to a report by the McKinsey Global Institute, as many as 375 million workers (or roughly 14% of the global workforce) may need to switch occupational categories by 2030 due to automation and other technological advancements. Furthermore, the report states that automation and other factors could displace up to 800 million jobs worldwide, highlighting the need for individuals to be agile and adaptable in their career paths.[24]

Most people I know, and indeed every person who calls me, reach out for career advice and counseling when they encounter the kind of situations that Shane and Mohammad encountered in their careers. Most often, they get good advice from whoever they contact, but they would undoubtedly have been in a significantly stronger position and mindset had they had the necessary career-building and navigation power skills. I also wonder how many wonderful

---

24 J Manyika, et al., 'Jobs Lost, Jobs Gained: Workforce transitions in a time of automation', (McKinsey Global Institute, December 2017), www.mckinsey.com/~/media/mckinsey/industries/public and social sector/our insights/what the future of work will mean for jobs skills and wages/mgi-jobs-lost-jobs-gained-executive-summary-december-6-2017.pdf, accessed 19 July 2023

career opportunities brushed passed them without them actively taking charge of their careers because they did not have these skills.

The five critical skills that you absolutely need to build and navigate an extraordinary career in the current and future world of work are:

1. Mastering the skill of creating impact
2. Stacking meaningful experiences
3. Performance leverage advantage
4. Reskilling and upskilling for career relevancy
5. Connecting today with your future by taking action

Mastering the skill of creating impact

In almost every coaching conversation with my clients, we discuss 'creating an impact' as a means and measure of moving forwards and growing in your career. If you want to advance in your career, you must seek opportunities to create more impact in your organization, function, team or job. Impact accelerates your growth and career trajectory. You must learn to assess and understand your impact at any point in your career and how you can increase it.

To achieve that, you must first understand what is essential to the organization, function, team or your job and then recognize how you impact that. For example, if one of the current key growth strategies of your company is digitalization, assess how you impact that strategy and what kind of contributions you can make towards the success of the digitalization strategy to increase your impact. Don't restrict yourself to a job description. Volunteer for projects or assignments related to that strategy. Seek opportunities to contribute to the top five strategies of your company, function or team.

In 2002, the Gillette Company was undergoing a worldwide transformation. A new CEO had been appointed and he identified three strategies that would deliver the transformation over the following three years or so. I was new in my post of VP of Corporate HR at the corporate headquarters in Boston, and my role supported five leaders in the C-suite reporting to the CEO. My job obviously had the opportunity to impact the three critical transformation strategies. I knew this was my opportunity to create the highest level of impact thus far in my career, working with the senior executives of the iconic global company and having exposure to the company's CEO. I made those three strategies the most important part of my job, understanding what they meant for each of the five functions I supported and how I impacted them. Needless to say, this exposed some learning and development areas for me, but it also gave me unbelievable exposure and visibility. I developed an excellent web of networks across the leadership team and the various parts of the organization. At the time, this was precisely what career success and fulfillment meant for me.

Once you understand the power of creating impact, it becomes easier to understand which job you want next and what learning and development you need. You then step into the next zone of impact, which is when impact leads to the kind of career success and fulfillment you aspire to. Your ability to make a significant and meaningful impact in your work will lead to:

1. Recognition: You are more likely to be recognized for your achievements by your leaders, peers and other stakeholders, leading to opportunities for promotion, raises or other rewards.

2. Reputation: Building a reputation for excellence and impact can help you stand out in your field and make it easier for you to advance your career.

3. Networking: Creating impact can also help you build your network, leading to new opportunities for collaboration, mentorship and career advancement.

4. Personal growth: Pushing yourself to create increasingly more impact, you can develop new skills, take on new challenges and grow.

Stacking meaningful experiences

The second piece of advice I give to everyone wanting to grow and develop in their careers at an accelerated pace is to seek diversified experiences. Experiences stretch you in terms of learning and growing and allow you to demonstrate your impact. I have had many pivotal experiences in my career. Each experience stretched me, got me out of my comfort zone, taught me things I did not know, built new connections, provided me with a deeper understanding of various parts of the organization, and allowed me to show my impact on matters important to the company.

Sometimes as employees, we wish things would normalize and that change would stop briefly, but if you are pursuing accelerated growth, seek diverse experiences and show up in those moments. Particularly explore jobs that give you diverse experiences which will build your development and allow an increasingly higher impact. These kinds of meaningful experiences will provide you with:

- Skill development
- An expanded network
- Opportunities to demonstrate initiative and drive
- A broadened perspective and adaptability
- Increased confidence and personal growth
- Transferable skills and versatility

It's important to note that the key lies in not only accumulating experiences, but also reflecting on them, extracting what you learned and applying those learnings to future projects, initiatives and jobs. This deliberate approach helps you grow continuously and accelerates your career development.

Performance leverage advantage

To build an extraordinary career, thinking strategically about performance is important. No matter what the situation you are in, do not let your performance drop. It does not matter if you do not like your company, its culture, its leadership or your boss. Keep your performance from slipping up. Your performance is on you. You need this mindset or power throughout your career. Do not give anyone any excuse to point towards your performance. If your performance is excellent, you start at a great place, no matter the situation. If you are in a job, do it well until you leave it.

Here are a few things to consider:

- Set ambitious goals that challenge you to stretch beyond your comfort zone and push yourself to perform at your best.
- Focus on continuous performance improvement by seeking opportunities to learn and grow.

- Adopt a growth mindset, believing that your abilities and intelligence are not fixed and can be developed further.
- Always look for opportunities to take initiative and go above and beyond your job description. Volunteer for new projects, suggest process improvements or take on additional responsibilities.
- Focus on delivering results. You must be seen as someone who consistently delivers results and can be counted on to deliver under pressure.

There is no question that in today's turbulent work and business landscape, you will face adversity, challenges and complexity in your career. How will you still maintain a high level of personal performance then? Here are a few things you can employ to navigate these difficulties and strive for excellence:

- Building resilience is crucial for facing adversity. Train yourself to see challenges as opportunities for learning and growth. Embrace adversity as temporary and focus on finding solutions.
- Learn to adapt to change.
- Prioritize self-care. Taking care of oneself is essential for sustained high performance. Prioritize physical exercise, adequate sleep and healthy eating habits. Engage in activities that

provide relaxation, reduce stress levels and maintain mental wellbeing.

- Stay focused. Concentrating on what truly matters avoids distraction and enhances performance.
- Reach out for support and collaborate with others.

No matter the circumstances, do not let your performance leverage slip away.

Reskilling and upskilling for career relevancy

Given the changes in the world of work, the demand for new capabilities and skills has increased significantly and will continue to grow. By 2025, the World Economic Forum projects up to 85 million jobs could be displaced by a shift in the division of labor between machines and humans. At the same time, 97 million new roles are expected to be created, driven by technological advances and continuous digital transformation.[25] Even for the talent that can remain in the same roles, the predicted share of core skills that will change is 40%. This means that no matter what job,

---

25 World Economic Forum, 'The Future of Jobs Report 2020', (World Economic Forum, October 2020), www3.weforum.org/docs/WEF_Future_of_Jobs_2020.pdf, accessed 13 July 2023

function or company you will work for, there will be a need for reskilling and upskilling.

According to the Cambridge Dictionary, upskilling is learning new skills or teaching workers new skills. Reskilling is, 'The process of learning new skills so you can do a different job or train people to do a different job.'[26] The question is, how do you go about upskilling and reskilling in your career? Here are some tips:

- Excel at understanding your skillset and act to build on the gaps you see.

- Find learning opportunities. There are many ways to learn new skills, including formal education, online courses, workshops, conferences, on-the-job training and networking.

- Learn how to unlearn. This is difficult because it's hard to unlearn what has contributed to our success. I constantly focus on the value I need to deliver and question my skills. I enjoy debating ideas on providing value, which allows me to see other ways to do things.

- Stay curious. An essential factor in upskilling and reskilling yourself is to stay curious. Develop the drive to learn and explore new things, be open to new ideas and seek out challenges that push you out of your comfort zone.

---

26 Cambridge Dictionary, https://dictionary.cambridge.org/dictionary/english/reskilling, accessed 19 June 2023

Looking back at my career thus far, it has been full of changes that have exposed me to new situations, scenarios, people, companies, leaders and jobs globally. A lot of it was not by design, but it required me to constantly learn new skills and build new relationships, which has eventually become my norm. Every eighteen months or so, I was in a new job, company, geography, or industry. Where I stayed longer than eighteen months, there was tremendous transformation. All this change has taught me how to:

- Develop new skills and knowledge quickly
- Unlearn and relearn quickly
- Anticipate, and prepare for, future events
- Build trusting relationships

Connecting today with your future by taking action

One of the most important differences between those who can build successful careers and those who don't is the simple but critical step of 'taking action'. I have seen numerous people being stuck in their careers because, for some reason or the other, they get stuck and do not take any action toward changing their career circumstances. Sometimes they get stuck in planning the best career plan, waiting for the perfect timing, do not have the courage to force the change, or cannot bring themselves to take a risk.

This book is about helping you create a thoughtful and purposeful plan for your career, but if you only plan, what good will it achieve? The best way to achieve your plan is to balance introspection and action. As you identify each step that you need to take to reach your goals, be aware of what you are learning about your plan and keep adjusting it based on what you pick up through your action steps. Real change comes from action. The distance between where you stand today and your career aspirations can only be bridged by your actions.

Summary

The five power skills listed in this chapter are critical to have throughout your career if you want to build and navigate an extraordinary career. These skills will enable to you to deal with adversity, pivot to new opportunities, transfer and learn new skills, maintain your passion for your work, not be stuck in the wrong job and reinvent yourself in your career when you need to. These skills will enable you to take charge of your career and hopefully achieve the success and fulfillment you aspire to.

SIX
Your Career Development Plan

The previous chapters of the book laid out the current trends and landscape of work that impact careers, and the strategies, skills and mindset needed to construct an extraordinary career. This chapter is about putting it all together into a clear career development plan that leads to actionable steps and success.

I will share with you a framework that you can use to write your career development plan. The essential purpose of the framework is to align your career aspirations with the actions you need to take to succeed and help you take control of your career. The framework assumes that you have the done the work mentioned in the previous chapters and that you now know yourself much better and also know the challenges and opportunities in front of you.

Let me start with a short story. I recently had a great career discussion with a young woman called Sally regarding her current career and aspirations. We'd had several conversations up to this point and this discussion focused on where she stood regarding her next steps. She's had a decent career in banking thus far, but has developed a strong interest in starting a business, one in which she has a great skillset that she has used to help many people as a hobby. Sally has also recently come to realize that the bank does not value her as it should. Looking at her peer group and the market, she feels she is significantly behind.

Based on her aspirations and our discussions, Sally is contemplating a career pivot from banking to starting her own business. This is on the back of some great thinking and sincere self-reflection on her part for several months. In this conversation, I aimed to outline some actionable next steps with her. As the conversation progressed, Sally revealed all the concerns holding her back from making a decision. She felt that she needed more time. I coached Sally to reframe her thinking regarding her career pivot decision. Instead of thinking, 'When will I make the decision?' and thus making it about time, I encouraged her to make it, 'What will get me ready to make a decision?'

Bank career   **Own business**

● Point B

What will get me ready to make a decision

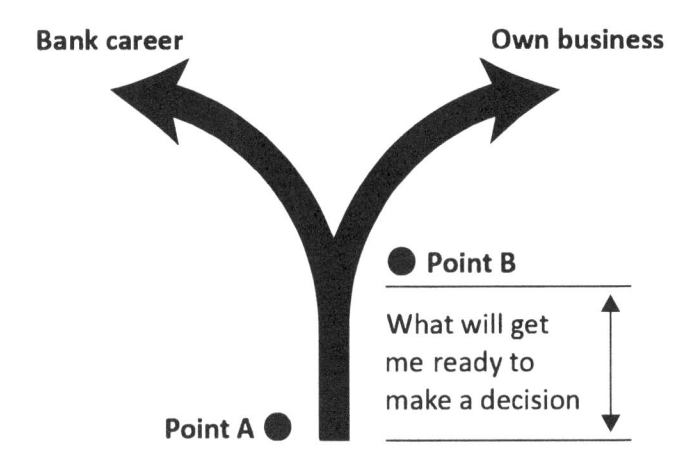

Point A ●

Sally was looking at the situation as if she had reached a career fork and now needed to choose between banking and starting her business, but she had not reached the fork yet. She was at point A, and not at point B, the fork in the road where she must make the decision. In our coaching session we focused on what would get her to point B. This reframed thinking helped Sally feel good immediately. She felt as though she was in control and would be better prepared once she reached the fork, versus having to make a daunting decision immediately.

I share this story because you will face many challenges, opportunities and turns in your career journey. If you do not have a clear and written career plan, you will likely make sub-optimal career decisions. A lot of reflection and work goes into writing a good career development plan, and it is a crucial step in your professional journey. Without a career plan, you risk drifting aimlessly through your career, lacking direction and purpose. Sally lacked a clearly defined plan and, as a result, did not feel ready to decide. By default, she continued choosing banking over starting her own business – a sub-optimal career decision. This is not uncommon; I have met many individuals who continue to make career decisions knowingly (and unknowingly) that are not optimal because they do not have a plan.

In my discussion with Sally, pointing out that she needed the plan to go from point A (where she stands today) to point B (where she can make a decision), helped her feel in control. A well-crafted career plan allows you to create a plan of action to achieve your goals and a roadmap to success. That is what Sally is working on now. A written plan connects your daily, weekly and monthly actions to your career aspiration, increasing the probability of your success significantly.

Your career development plan needs to include your:

1. Career aspirations
2. Long- and short-term goals
3. Strengths and areas of improvement (2:1 ratio)
4. Action steps

This list describes the different elements of the career development framework I recommend using. It has four essential ingredients and is simple and effective. Let's go through them.

Career aspiration

In Chapter 3, we briefly discussed knowing and following your career aspiration. Your aspiration lies at the intersection of your talent, your passion and the needs of other people. In this chapter, we will talk about writing your career aspiration as a first step of your career development plan. It is the anchor that determines everything else that goes into your plan. Without knowing your aspiration, identifying any action steps towards career development is like taking a shot in the dark and hoping you hit something. Many professionals struggle to find their career aspirations and therefore lack direction, purpose and fulfillment in their careers.

Discovering your career aspiration allows you to set specific goals and work towards them, which will help you to focus your energy and time, making you more efficient in your pursuits.

Secondly, discovering your career aspiration allows you to make informed decisions about your future. When you know what you want to achieve, you can make choices that align with your goals. This enables you to make informed decisions that can positively impact your future.

Thirdly, discovering your career aspiration helps you to build a fulfilling career. When you pursue a career that aligns with your interests, talents and passions, you are more likely to find meaning and satisfaction in your work. This, in turn, can lead to higher job satisfaction, improved mental health and a sense of fulfillment in life. When you enjoy your work, you are more likely to be successful, as you are willing to put in the effort and time required to excel in your field.

Discovering your career aspiration is essential for achieving a fulfilling and successful career. Take the time to explore your interests, talents and passions and discover what you want to achieve professionally. Here are some important tips on writing your career aspiration:

1. Do not try to make it perfect. Write something and continue to refine it. I have observed many people getting stuck because they try to write the perfect career aspiration.

2. Your career aspiration statement is for you, not for anyone else. It must make sense to you, not necessarily others.

3. Career aspiration is a high-level statement that says who you are and what success looks like in your career.

4. Revisit Chapter 2, where we discussed what career success and fulfillment looks like to you and the work we did on your values. Use that to articulate your aspiration.

5. It should be meaningful to you, motivational, far in the future, authentic with a dose of realism in it and appeal to your head and heart.

YOUR CAREER DEVELOPMENT PLAN

6. In writing mine, over time I got comfortable with 'go big, or go home'.

7. It's the 'why' of your career journey.

8. It is not a goal or a roadmap.

Let me show you how I kept on refining my career aspiration statements from 2008 to 2010. I believe these statements are responsible for my success, leading me to the pinnacle of my profession. Note that these statements captured where I was in my career at that time: what I wanted, what fulfilled me and what resonated with me. These statements were for me, and they very quickly incorporated my 'whole self' and not just my 'work self'.

In 2008, my career aspiration read: *To be an outstanding HR Leader who is able to impact and influence the business in a big way through his contributions, with a continued upwards career progression.*

In 2009, I refined it to: *The future is within me, I am not going to wait for it to come to me, I am in control. Each day I will be all I can be for my family, friends, and Dun & Bradstreet (my company).*

In 2010, I rewrote it again: *My aspiration is to succeed in all aspects of my life. I will focus my energy and time on outcomes that are important in each area of my life. I will express my thoughts, opinions and ideas more openly, more often and without trepidation. I have a lot to give to life and people around me. I will not hold back anything, and I will not wait for the perfect moment to do it. Values will always be at the forefront of all I do. I will share my enthusiasm and passion for doing the right things.*

What is your career aspiration?

Long- and short-term goals

Once you have written down your career aspiration, the next step is to write down long- and short-term goals that move you towards your aspiration.

Long-term goals are typically those that will take you several years to achieve. They should be specific, measurable, achievable, relevant and time-bound (SMART). For example, a long-term goal might be for you to write and publish five books within the next ten years, with each book being at least 200 pages long and receiving positive reviews from readers. But this must link to, and help you achieve, your career aspiration.

Short-term goals are those that can be achieved within a shorter timeframe, typically weeks or months. These goals should help you make progress towards achieving your long-term goals and should also be SMART. For example, a short-term goal might be to write at least 1,000 words each day for the next two weeks, or to attend a writing workshop within the next month to improve your writing skills.

By setting and achieving short-term goals, you build momentum and confidence, which can help you stay motivated and focused on your long-term goals and your career aspiration.

It's important to strike a balance between the two. Focusing too much on long-term goals can be overwhelming and discouraging if progress is slow, while focusing too much on short-term goals can lead to losing sight of the bigger picture and direction of your career. It's important to regularly reassess your long-term goals and adjust your short-term goals to ensure that you're making progress towards achieving them.

Let me share part of my goals that correspond to my 2010 aspiration I shared earlier in this chapter:

- Short-term goal: Become Head of HR of a company in 2–3 years
- Long-term goal: Be able to retire at the age of fifty-five and help and inspire others to succeed

Strengths and areas of improvement (2:1 ratio)

Once you have written down your long- and short-term goals, the next step is deciding which strengths you will leverage and which areas of improvement you are going to work on to achieve your goals.

Before beginning this part of writing your career development plan, let me share this brief story. In the early part of my career, I approached everyone about my performance review discussions with the same mindset. My leader explained what I did well, and I did not care much about that because I was waiting for the part of the discussion where we discussed where I had to improve. I was so focused on learning, growing, and performing well, and the only way for me to do that (or so I thought), was by improving in areas where I had not done well. I glossed over any strength that was identified and focused on my areas of improvement. If someone had asked me at that time what my strengths were, I would not have been able to identify any strength with conviction. I never focused on my strengths, never identified them, and, therefore, never thought of leveraging them.

It was not until I started writing meaningful career aspirations that I realized that I was missing a significant growth driver: identifying and leveraging my strengths. I realized that to achieve my career aspiration, I must leverage my strengths in addition to improving in areas where I needed improvement. This was a much quicker path to success. In fact, I tilted the balance and discovered the '2:1 ratio' principle. My career development plans identified strengths and areas of improvement in 2:1 ratio. My 'aha' moment was that writing my career development plan was about making progress towards my career aspiration, and I believe you get there faster by leveraging your strengths more than your areas of improvement. Just focusing on improving in certain areas does not necessarily mean you are making progress towards your career aspiration.

Hence, if you identify two strengths that you want to leverage to accomplish your goals, then identify one area of improvement.

Identifying and leveraging your strengths

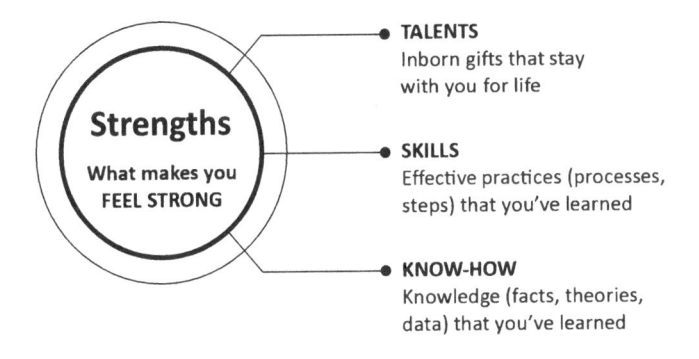

Strengths
What makes you
FEEL STRONG

- **TALENTS**
  Inborn gifts that stay with you for life
- **SKILLS**
  Effective practices (processes, steps) that you've learned
- **KNOW-HOW**
  Knowledge (facts, theories, data) that you've learned

The first step in leveraging your strengths is to identify what they are. Your strengths are an amalgamation of your natural talents, skills, knowledge and traits that you excel in and enjoy doing. It is important to note that although we all have multiple strengths in many areas of our life, you are only looking at strengths that you will leverage to get closer to your career aspirations and milestones here. As an example, if Usain Bolt, the fastest man in the world, identified speed, collaboration, mental resilience, good math skills and compassion as his strengths, he wouldn't leverage all of them to win the gold medal in the next summer Olympics. Here are some ways to identify strengths to enhance careers:

- **Self-reflection:** Spend some time reflecting on your past experiences and accomplishments. What tasks did you enjoy doing the most? What activities come naturally to you? What do you receive compliments for? Answering these questions can help you identify your strengths.

- **Feedback:** Seek feedback from colleagues, friends, family members and mentors. They can offer an outside perspective on your strengths and help you identify areas where you excel.

- **Strengths assessments:** Consider taking a strengths assessment, such as CliftonStrengths™. These assessments provide insights into your unique strengths and can help you identify areas where you can excel in your career.

- **Performance evaluations:** Ask your supervisor for performance evaluations to get a better understanding of your strengths and areas where you need improvement.

By utilizing these methods, you can identify your strengths and begin to leverage them to enhance your career.

Identifying areas of improvement

Working on improving yourself in critical areas is important, but it cannot be the entire focus of your plan. Include only those areas of improvement that are critical to helping you achieve your career aspiration. Here are some ways to identify areas of improvement:

- **Seek feedback:** Ask colleagues, supervisors and mentors for feedback on areas where you can improve. Constructive feedback can be instrumental in identifying blind spots and areas where you may need to focus your attention.

- **Conduct a self-assessment:** Do a self-assessment of your skills, knowledge and areas of weakness. Be honest with yourself about where you need improvement and set specific goals to address these areas. Consider the skills required for your current position, as well as skills that may be required for future roles.

- **Analyze performance evaluations:** Examine past performance evaluations to identify areas where you have received feedback for improvement.

- **Learn from mistakes:** Analyze what went wrong and identify what could have been done differently.

Action steps

This part of your development plan is about the activities you will undertake to achieve your long- and short-term goals. There are several reasons why people may feel stuck in their careers and not take any action towards their aspirations, but if you follow the steps outlined so far, you will get:

- **Clarity:** One of the biggest reasons why people don't pursue their aspirations is because they don't have a clear idea of what they want. Without a clear goal in mind, it's difficult to take the necessary steps to get there.

- **Courage and resilience:** Fear of failure is another common reason why people don't pursue their aspirations. They may feel that they will not succeed, and so do not even try. A meaningful career development plan will provide you with courage and resilience.

- **Confidence:** Lack of confidence can also hold people back from pursuing their aspirations. A good career development plan will give you the confidence that you need.

Action steps are specific steps that you must plan. They can be on a daily, weekly or monthly basis (or as and when required) and are intended to leverage your strengths and help you to improve in certain areas.

Summary

In this chapter, I have described how you can write a meaningful and impactful career development plan. I have seen many people who seem to be 'sleepwalking' through their careers without taking any action towards their aspirations. This can be a frustrating and disheartening experience, especially for those who have a clear idea of what they want to achieve, but are unable to take the necessary steps to get there.

I sincerely and strongly advise you to write a career development plan for yourself by doing your homework and then keep refining it as you continue to learn what works and what does not. It took me a few iterations to write one that hit the mark for me.

SEVEN
Important Career Conversations

This last chapter is all about the importance of career conversations. At different points in my career, I was lucky to have insightful and meaningful conversations with leaders and others that changed my perspective and career trajectory. Somewhere within me, I was looking for these perspectives and advice, and so I landed in the right place, talking to the right person. Hence, I am writing this chapter to strongly encourage you to seek these conversations throughout your career and not leave it to luck or chance. Take advantage of this. One good conversation can shift the direction of your career forever.

Throughout this book, I have highlighted that the career landscape is about rapid change. You will face many challenges, opportunities, and choices that require you to know yourself and have insightful and meaningful career conversations with someone at the right time. Research data suggests that despite the benefits of career conversations, many individuals need to seek out, or engage in, these discussions. Similarly, my experience covering numerous meetings with employees across the globe tells me that these insightful conversations are only taking place for some people. Whatever the reason for this lack of engagement, you must seek these career conversations to truly take charge of your career.

The four types of career conversations

There are four types of the conversations you must seek:

1. Early career conversations

2. Career development and growth conversations

3. Performance review conversations

4. Salary increase conversations

1. Early career conversations

Early in our careers, there is much to think about and look forward to. Whether we choose a profession aligned with our educational background or not, many factors influence our decisions and we face numerous challenges and concerns presented by the changing economic and job landscape. Without proper guidance, challenges such as economic uncertainty, lack of experience, pressure from family or society, lack of clarity and self-awareness or balancing work and life can lead to uncertainty and indecision and make it difficult for young professionals to make informed career decisions. Years later, a vast majority of these young professionals are not happy, successful or fulfilled in their careers. You must seek early career conversations to gain clarity and confidence in your decisions and navigate these challenges successfully.

As a child, I wanted to be a pilot. As a teenager, I was determined to be a cricket player. Entering college, I thought engineering was what I needed as a career. I dropped out of engineering and felt that my calling was an MBA and a marketing career. I ended up with a lifelong career in Human Resources because of that one pivotal career conversation I had with my manager at Exxon, which resonated with me. I was not seeking that conversation per se, but it happened at the right time for me and provided me the clarity I needed.

Having just completed my MBA, I began preparing for interviewing for marketing jobs – the profession I thought I wanted. At the same time, Exxon came to our campus and asked the graduating class to take an aptitude test as they wanted to recruit candidates for various jobs in the company. My entire class took that test. Based on the test results, the company called me a few days later and said they would like to offer me a job in the HR department. I had no inclination or interest in HR at that time. I accepted the position as my father convinced me that it was a good company, and after a few months, I could request a transfer to marketing. They were also offering a salary that was higher than the offers most of my classmates had received.

I reported to the Training and Development Manager of the company, who was an outstanding leader. I was unsure when to have a 'transfer to marketing' conversation with him, but in my second week, he decided to talk with me about my career. The critical message that struck a massive chord with me in that career conversation was that there were only a few MBAs in the HR field at that point in time. The function was considered an administrative and a policing function in Pakistan, so many people from the army and police joined, as they had administrative and policy-implementation experience. However, the HR function was moving towards a transformation where it would be asked to add more business value. He said that in this new HR function, I would stand out in the HR profession because of my business degree and ability to add value. This conversation instantly changed my perspective on HR and how I could succeed and make a difference. I never looked back. This little nugget of adding 'business' value is the essence of any successful HR career. That one conversation helped me understand it and clarified how to proceed with my career. Now, imagine if I had never had this conversation. I may not have ever known what I was really seeking, and I would have just focused on getting a transfer into marketing.

Seek these early career conversations with the following mindset:

1. Aim to get clarity on what resonates with you at that time at a deep level. The conversations should be about what is happening in your profession, where it is headed and what it takes to succeed in it. You're looking for alignment between the profession's requirements and what you want to do.

2. Approach the conversations with a curiosity mindset. Show a willingness to explore new thinking and ideas, ask questions that peel the onion further, and seek new knowledge. Look for information that helps you decide your career goals, the path to progress, learning and fulfillment.

3. Your mindset should be that nothing is written in stone. You can change your direction, goals and path. Don't rely on preconceived notions or assumptions.

Choosing the right person to have this conversation with is also essential. It can be your supervisor, a leader, HR or a coach. Be bold about seeking several individuals and exchanges. I look for these factors in that person/s:

- Someone who has relevant experience
- Someone whose career trajectory you admire

- Someone you feel comfortable with
- Someone who is recommended by a person in a similar situation as yours

2. Career development and growth conversations

The second kind of conversation I highly encourage you to seek is career development and growth discussions. These are not your regular performance review discussions. These are intentional conversations you should have with your manager, HR, mentor or colleagues about your career aspirations, long- and short-term career goals and growth opportunities.

Let me share an example with you. By 2008, I had a successful career in HR, having worked for prestigious blue chip organizations with iconic brands, and had been promoted within those organizations. I was learning and growing in my profession. I lived in a good area of New Jersey, USA, my family was doing well and I was thankful. I was thriving by all career measurements at the time. After all, imagine a person who grew up and was educated in Pakistan, who started as a trainee and grew to the position of VP in a global company like the Gillette Company, and was now working as VP of HR in another 150-plus-year-old company which was publicly listed on the stock exchange, with four former US presidents having worked for them (including Abraham Lincoln). This was more than I had ever imagined for my career.

I had been with this company for just over a year and was looking forward to discussing my leadership development plan (LDP) with my boss – one that every employee would have around that time of the year regarding their career. My boss, Patti Clifford, was passionate about and extremely good at these conversations. In preparing for the discussion, my mindset was open and transparent, as I trusted Patti and knew she had my and the company's best interest in mind. I expected to come out of the meeting with meaningful strengths that I could leverage and areas of improvement to focus on to progress my career. The meeting took place, and it was fantastic. I came out of it with much more than I had expected. Through the conversation, Patti helped me unlock my potential. Even with significant progress in my career up to that point, I had not considered my full potential, and I had unknowingly set a limit for myself. It was another pivotal moment in my career, and it happened because of an excellent career development conversation with my boss.

During the conversation, Patti asked me what my career aspiration was then. As I stated earlier, I was happy with my career progress, so my answer was, 'I want to continue to learn and grow and assume positions of increasing responsibility.' Her next question threw me off. She asked me if I had ever thought of being the Head of HR of the company. I had not, and she asked me why. I didn't know the answer to that question. Why didn't I think about being the Head of

HR of this company, or any other company? It's a pinnacle position in the career of any HR professional. I gave Patti a useless answer, and she asked me to go home and think about the 'why' questions.

I reflected deeply on the question. I realized that I had formed a limiting belief that no US/global company would make me their Head of HR because of where I came from, my appearance and my accent. I did not fit the mold of the Head of HR. Others would always be better than me. We all form these self-limiting beliefs because of various factors. When I told Patti about this, she quickly helped me dismantle this belief. First, nobody had told me I could not be the Head of HR. So, recognizing that I had this limiting belief by itself helped me. Second, we focused on what it would take for me to be the Head of HR of the company, which helped me bring it into my realm of possibilities. These discussions left me energized, with clear direction and a plan: the essence of a significant career development and growth conversation. Less than two years later, I was the Head of HR of the company. I will never be able to thank Patti enough.

You must seek these conversations regularly in your career. Here are some tips when seeking these conversations:

- The best kind of career development conversations are going to help you unlock and maximize your potential.

- Most managers and leaders need to be more experienced or trained to have these conversations. That does not mean you do not seek them.

- Do not treat these conversations as feedback sessions. Prepare for them and bring your thinking, your challenges and the opportunities that you see to these meetings. Seek other perspectives and viewpoints.

- Remember from the previous chapter, the aim of these conversations is to seek diversity of experiences and delivery of increasing levels of impact. Explore opportunities for lateral or vertical moves, discuss potential projects or assignments and seek advice on progressing in your career.

3. Performance review conversations

Very early on in my career, I understood that my performance is the key to the leverage I want to have in my career. If my performance is assessed to be below expectations, nothing else will matter concerning my career. Good boss, bad boss, good company, bad company, poor economy, good economy, no matter what – from the moment I understood the concept of performance leverage, I have always wanted my performance to be above average at the least. I strongly recommend this mindset.

I therefore approached my performance review conversations with the ultimate outcome being that of delivering above-average performance. None of us are guaranteed a good boss, company, culture or performance review process. But the outcome we seek remains the same: delivering excellent performance. I encourage you to ensure that you get what you want from your performance review conversations. As an employee, you have a significant role in creating a supportive environment for constructive and positive performance review discussions. Imagine me reacting to my leader giving me feedback in a negative manner by challenging my leader's assessment, sulking, throwing a tantrum and generally not being open to input. What does that teach my leader about giving me any feedback in the future?

Create an environment where a meaningful and constructive conversation can occur. I am not suggesting that you do not express your point of view or disagreement in these conversations. I am suggesting you have an open and honest dialogue constructively, always remembering that you want to deliver above-par performance. Consider the following for these conversations to be constructive, enabling you to deliver your performance goals:

- Create an environment where you and your leader can have open and transparent conversations about how you are doing and what is expected of you.

- Don't just wait for the official, company-designated times for these conversations. Have conversations as and when they are needed.
- If you have not done something well, admit it and seek advice on how to move forwards.
- Share what you have learned.
- Disagree where you need to, but with specifics.
- Approach the conversations not as a process, but as an outcome-enabling step.

In my entire career, I had one performance review where I was rated below par, leading to easily my worst performance review discussion. It happened a year into being promoted as the Head of HR for the first time in my career. A lot went wrong there. Looking back, here is how I see it:

- I could have built a better relationship with my leader throughout the year. I disagreed with him on many matters and did not respect him. This led me to a biased assessment of my performance, focusing on what my boss might think and how I wanted to defend it. At the same time, I chose to underrate myself on specific goals to show I was being balanced.
- The conversation itself was horrendous. I did not control my emotions as I would have liked.
- Leaving the conversation, I took away nothing constructive, with little to look forward to.

I ended up leaving that organization soon after, but with several lessons learned. There were things that I was not going to repeat and things I would absolutely do, but the biggest mistake that I allowed was letting my performance be rated below expectations. I did some great work on the things I cared about but did not align 100% on other goals with my leader. I can blame others and other things, but looking back, I did not create the performance leverage I should have. I share this with you to bring my point home.

4. Salary increase conversations

Have you ever asked for a salary increase? How did that conversation go? At some point in your career, you will likely consider having a salary increase conversation. For most people, these conversations are not easy and, in fact, can be nerve-wracking. However, they are essential to your career progression, success and fulfillment. Whether it's a fear of being rejected, a lack of confidence in your abilities, a fear of damaging your relationship, or simply you expect the company to do its job and pay you what you deserve, you need to get comfortable and confident in having these conversations. With all the changes in the world of work, compensation systems and practices will continue to be in a state of flux and catching up. You will need to advocate for yourself.

Of course, there are certain ways to go about it. I remember a supply chain director attending a

IMPORTANT CAREER CONVERSATIONS

meeting with the company's CEO with a seven-year graph projection of his compensation, accounting for inflation and above-par performance in each of the seven years. The CEO was not expecting a compensation discussion, let alone approving a self-generated seven-year salary projection for the director. This approach is clearly not recommended. I also remember a Finance Manager reviewing particular job adverts and approaching his boss, saying he was paid below the market. That's not the way to go, either. A friend in New York has been accepting of the explanations given by various leaders in her company that they are restricted in their budget while giving her high praise and low salary increments over the last decade. She is now significantly behind her peers. This is also not the way to go. Here are my recommendations on how to have this conversation:

- Do not approach it as a 'one and done' conversation. You need to engage your leader on this topic through **various discussions** that help your leader understand how you feel about your compensation and why, while letting your leader provide you with their perspective.

- You should **research** the market from time to time and have a good handle on where your compensation stands versus the market or your peers. Don't just do it at the time of a compensation review. This will give you confidence.

- Make a list of the **results** you have achieved, where you have gone above and beyond, where you have taken on additional responsibility, and how you have helped others succeed. This will help you articulate the value you bring.
- **Follow up** on your conversation with a thank you note.

If the increase is smaller than you think it should be, engage your leader in a further conversation that helps you understand how you can get your compensation to be where you think it should be. If your request is denied, take some time to try and understand the reasons why and if there is anything you can do to alter them.

Summary

During your career, you will encounter many different conversations impacting your career. I have picked the above four as the most important based on my own experience and the numerous conversations I have had with professionals across the globe.

In my view, conversations early in your career that give you clarity and direction, conversations that help unlock and maximize your potential, conversations that lead to performance leverage and conversations related to your salary increases will have the most significant impact on your career success and fulfillment.

The advice given here can also be applied to other career conversations of importance you might have.

What are the most insightful conversations that have significantly and positively impacted your career so far, and what did you learn from these discussions?

Conclusion

I am glad that you have reached the end of the book. As it suggests, attaining extraordinary career success and fulfillment requires a lot of work and a strong will and commitment, but the ultimate payoff is worth it. If you follow the advice and strategies in the book, creating an extraordinary career is well within your reach. Everything in this book is real, tried and tested. Take a little time to reflect and absorb what you have learned here and let it become part of how you think about your career. You will unlock your career potential.

In essence, *Careers Unleashed* gets you to take charge of your career. No matter what you choose, your career journey will present challenges, highs and lows, changes and opportunities. Taking charge means how you respond to these. It means finding purpose and direction in your work and doing meaningful work. It means how you deal with adversity and respond when things don't go your way. It means how you move forwards with momentum in your career and use your time at work. It means building the beliefs that help you succeed and creating the relationships and connections you need for your career. It means how you connect your todays with your career aspirations for the future. This book provides you with practical advice, guidance and examples for all of this to help you apply concepts and strategies that will enable you to break free from your limiting beliefs and unleash your full potential in your professional life.

This book has taught you to not wait for luck and success to fall into your lap. It has explained how to define career success and fulfillment by understanding yourself, your motivations and your expectations and not defining it through others' expectations or criteria. Your aspirations may change and evolve with time as you reach important milestones or as the world of work unfolds change. The clearer your aspirations are to you, the more confident you will be in making career decisions, managing your expectations and being more content. You will also start seeing more opportunities.

I have written this book to shift your mindset regarding career success and fulfillment and help you to unlock your career potential. However, my aim is

CONCLUSION

not just to motivate you in the moment, but to provide you with career-long strategies, skills and tips for your journey. Most importantly, it requires action on your part. Careers impact and contribute to almost every aspect of our lives. By acting on your career aspirations, you will make a substantial and lasting difference in your professional and personal life. As I mentioned earlier in the book, the most important difference between those who achieve their career aspirations and those who don't is that achievers act in line with their ambitions while others do not.

Seeing you make a massive difference in your career will give me immense fulfillment. Over time, I will be providing a host of additional resources on my website https://ahusain.consulting to continue to help you beyond this book. You can also see my posts on this subject on LinkedIn.

Remove the barriers holding you back and forge your career to great heights.

The Author

Asad Husain is a future-focused strategic HR leader passionate about inspiring and influencing people worldwide to achieve their career aspirations.

He is a four-time Head of HR with over thirty-one years of experience contributing to organizational growth and individual success for employees in blue chip companies like the Gillette Company, Proctor & Gamble, Dun & Bradstreet, Del Monte, Big Heart Pet Brands and C&S Wholesale Grocers.

He has lived and worked in the USA, UK, UAE, Russia and Pakistan and has held global responsibilities during his career.

This varied experience, the guidance of many good leaders and his continuous desire to learn and grow have enabled him to learn the art of building a successful career and unlocking potential. He is keen to share his global learnings to inspire success.

🌐 https://ahusain.consulting

in www.linkedin.com/in/husainasad

◎ inspiring_people_to_succeed

Made in the USA
Middletown, DE
10 October 2023